# Self-Publishing

*3 Manuscripts in 1 Book, Including: How to Self-Publish, How to Write Fiction and How to Write Non-Fiction*

Jaiden Pemton

# More by Jaiden Pemton

Discover all books from the Creative Writing Series by Jaiden Pemton at:

bit.ly/jaiden-pemton

Book 1: *How to Write Fiction*

Book 2: *How to Tell a Story*

Book 3: *How to Write a Screenplay*

Book 4: *How to Write Sales Copy*

Book 5: *How to Edit Writing*

Book 6: *How to Self-Publish*

Book 7: *How to Write Non-Fiction*

Book 8: *How to Write Content*

Themed book bundles available at discounted prices:

bit.ly/jaiden-pemton

# Copyright

---

# Table of Contents

# Book 1: How to Self-Publish

*7 Easy Steps to Master Self-Publishing, eBook Creation, Ghostwriting, Book Marketing & Publishing*

Jaiden Pemton

# Introduction

If you are starting with this guide, something has led you to consider self-publishing. You have probably heard of the liberation and total ownership of the self-publishing process, as well as the potential to earn more of your own money. If you are considering whether or how to take the leap into self-publishing, this guide is for you!

When it comes to self-publishing, you must be aware of the industry's ins and outs, the correct terminology to use, how to interact with editors, designers, your fans, network, and target audience, and potential retailers. In modern-day society, publishing is a more ambitious field than ever before, and you need to be on top of your game in order to thrive within it. Whether you're still wondering if self-publishing is for you, or you've already committed to the journey and just need to know where to go next, this guide will show you everything you need to know to thrive within the industry and make a name for yourself as a self-published author. Thank you for choosing to embark on this journey with us.

In order to be an effective self-publisher, you must be prepared to be thorough, intentional, and informed on every step of the journey. Self-publication requires an in-depth understanding of the industry, the genre you are writing in, how to check all the boxes in writing, editing, design, making necessary financial decisions, and marketing and distribution strategies to use.

With the writing industry becoming more challenging by the day, you must be willing to bring high energy to every step of the process. When you embark on the journey of self-publication, you must be clear-headed, driven in your goals, and ready to confront every logistic that comes your way. This guide will provide you with in-depth knowledge of each of these logistics, tactics for managing them, and how to keep your vision fresh in your mind throughout the process.

In this guide you will find a comprehensive step-by-step reference format with everything you need to know about the self-publication process. You will become familiar with the beginning and middle stages of the processes, as well as information to make marketing and distribution decisions at the end of the process. You will learn top secret tips and tricks for writing, editing, title generation, design, description writing, and publication logistics. You will understand how to use social media, build your fanbase, and maintain high audience engagement. Additionally, you will see easy-to-follow lists of key terms, secrets of success, and things to avoid.

The chapters of this guide will take you through each step of the self-publishing journey to help you check all of the necessary boxes and steer clear of any big mistakes. Each chapter is designed with astounding detail to help you stay on track and address any questions or concerns you have along the way. Regardless of where you're at on your self-publishing journey, this guide has all the tools you need to set yourself apart as an expert editor and is sure to serve as the perfect guide to revolutionize your editing experience.

Happy writing!

# Chapter 1: Step 1 - The Basic Components of Self-Publishing

There are several significant differences between self-publishing and traditional publishing. Before you make a set decision on which route to choose, it is essential to consider the elements of both. Traditional Publishing requires the use of an agent, a publisher to accept your manuscript, and a contract between the publisher and yourself that allows the publisher to purchase rights to your book. After the publisher has purchased rights, they will assume responsibility for all further editing, formatting, and designing. The money you earn will be dependent on how well the book sells once it has hit the market.

Although you will have to pay less for production expenses and have fewer responsibilities in terms of the fine details, this process is highly competitive and can take a great deal of time. You can expect plenty of rejections from agents and publishers, and even if you land one, you may lose your sense of agency and creative input in how the final project turns out. This means that the book can be designed and edited without your input. In addition, if your book does do well, you will not earn as much as you could earn if you had self-published.

**Benefits of Self-Publishing**

Although self-publishing requires a lot of work in terms of editing, design, and distribution and may require more money upfront, it is an excellent option if you want to avoid the roadblocks of rejection, loss of agency in your book production, and potential loss of money once it hits the market. In many cases, self-publishing is a great place to start getting your name out there and building a fanbase surrounding your work.

**Key Terminology**

Once you've chosen to begin the self-publishing journey, there are a number of critical elements you need to be aware of. The most basic of these elements are publishing terms, which you should be prepared to interact with often throughout the publishing process. While you may not encounter all of these terms, it is essential to understand what they mean.

· Barcode → an image that indicates the ISBN and, in some cases, the book's price. Barcodes are machine-readable and are often used by book retailers on print books.

· Copyright → the declaration that the creator has exclusive rights to the publication, distribution, and adaptation of their work during a certain period of time.

· Description → the part of the book that communicates to distribution partners and, later, potential customers what the book is about and how to market it.

· Distributor → the party designated to credit, fulfillment, collections, and in the book industry, selling, on behalf of a publisher.

· E-Retailer → a book retailer who works in an online space.

· Edition → version of a book, many times which has been re-released with corrections or new features.

· ISBN (International Standard Book Number) → Aa13-digit code provided by the ISBN agency of a particular country and assumed by a publisher to demonstrate the format, edition, and publication details of a work. ISBNs are used globally and help to identify book titles and format information quickly.

· .jpg or jpeg. → image files that are most effective for colorful images to be used in the book.

· Keywords → single words or phrases which can be used to summarize the book and make it easier to search for.

· Metadata → necessary information about the book like the price, cover, publication date, author, description, table of contents, etc. which is used by booksellers and buyers.

· On Sale Date → the date when retail partners can start selling a book.

· Page Count → the total number of pages in a book (always divisible by two), including blank pages.

· PDF → Adobe file format which allows for easy creation and sharing of documents that are easy and consistent to print.

· Publication Date → the date a book can be released to retail consumers or libraries to assume possession of.

· Publisher → the person who owns legal rights to the book and makes decisions regarding when it will be available.

· Retailer → any place that sells books (sourced from publishers, distributors, and wholesalers) to consumers.

· Returns → the ability for booksellers to return books to the publisher if they have too many or no longer have use for a particular book. Booksellers must charge publishers the purchase price of the book and will then be reimbursed.

· Status → indicates whether or not a book is available, using terms like "forthcoming," "active," or "publication canceled".

· Subject → used to place books into categories based on content.

· Suggested Retail Price → indication of the price by the publisher.

· Title → information used for reporting and reseller catalog communications.

· Trade → traditional bookselling channels like independent and chain bookstores.

· Wholesaler → a business that is dedicated to fulfilling orders for retailers and libraries with the books they obtain from publishers and distributors.

Although self-publishing can be a taxing process, you can expect to fully control the content and design, marketing, and edits. Your book will likely have increased longevity because no one gets to decide when to stop marketing it. The royalties you save from having to pay a publisher can go into your own pocket instead, and you have the freedom to change the price of your book whenever you want.

Additionally, you have a greater ability to distribute the book worldwide and be in full control of the rights granted to foreign publishers who may want to purchase rights to distribute in their country. Lastly, self-publishing gives you a great deal of flexibility regarding your work timeline and the deals you cut with outside organizations. All in all, self-publishing is a great route for writers looking for independence, agency, and flexibility in their publishing process.

# Chapter 2: Step 2 - Beginning Stages

The beginning stages of the self-publishing journey involves bringing your book into existence and getting the essential details underway. The three stages of this process are writing, editing, and generating a title. There are several tools available to help you throughout these processes.

**Writing your Book**

The first step of the self-publishing process is to write your book. Before you begin, you will need to determine the genre you are writing in. Consider the typical audience of this genre to decide who you are writing to. What kind of writing will pique their interest and keep them engaged? Be sure to pay attention to other relevant works in the genre, such as films, screenplays, and books by other authors, to inform yourself of what does best in the industry.

Writing from this place of understanding and inspiration can help you enjoy the process and ask yourself the critical question: *"What am I trying to say, and how can I say it in a way it hasn't been said before?"* You will need to take the necessary actions of character development, plot development, crafting setting, establishing style and voice, determining theme, making the experience personal, developing a shining moment, etc.

Before you begin to write, you should be able to narrow down what you are trying to say and what impact you want it to have on the readers. If you are writing a nonfiction book, you will need to carve out time to research your topic at great length to ensure credibility. If you are storytelling, you may need to experiment with various organizational techniques, central themes, points of view, and styles to find what works best for you and your goals. Be sure to give yourself space to take breaks, explore, and change things around throughout the writing process, without too much stress or rigidity. Remember, you will have the editing process to work things out any structural or copywriting errors.

## Finetuning the Work Through Editing

Although it is possible to edit your book on your own, many self-publishers choose to hire an editor to obtain an outsider's perspective and receive insight on details they may have missed. If you decide to hire an editor, be sure to find one who is comfortable and skilled in your genre. Editors with specialized skillsets can provide invaluable perspective and edits to your writing. Ask yourself what you are looking for in the editor. Do you need an editor who specializes in dialogue? Perhaps you are looking for one to pick apart your structure and organization to ensure good flow. Or, perhaps you need an editor who is skilled in mood development. Either way, make sure you know your editor's strengths, specialties, and comfort level with the material before hiring them.

**Making Use of the Editing Process for Your Career**

When you begin the editing process, you must bear in mind that this is about much more than the book in front of you. What you learn throughout this process is what you will take with you into the rest of your writing career, and it will help you formulate your future works while learning what to implement and what to avoid. The editing process is your chance to grow by looking back on what you have written reflectively, applying feedback, and developing your writing craft.

If you choose to invest in an editor or editing team, you can consider it an investment in your learning and, ultimately, your future success in writing. Over time, you will see your style, voice, and general writing skill improve. Working with an editor is one of the most remarkable ways to see this transformation happen and may even lead you to create new editions of previous works.

**Understanding the Stages of Editing**

Before you begin the editing process, you need to know which type of editing you need. There are three stages of the editing process, which are vastly different from each other and all equally important. The first stage of editing is the structural or developmental stage. You determine the big picture of the story and determine if the organization flows well enough to represent that big picture. The following stage is the line editing stage, which is where you begin to narrow the scope, finetuning the language, and making as many smaller edits as possible. This is a stage for a lot of experiments with moving things around, adding new (but relevant) information, or removing parts of the book altogether.

The next part of stage two is copyediting, which involves acute attention to things like spelling, punctuation, grammar, and passive voice. The third stage of editing is the proofreading stage, where you will give the work a few final passes to pick up any errors that may have been overlooked. In many cases, it's a good idea to hire a different editor for each of the three stages so that you can take advantage of their unique skillsets and avoid the risk of them becoming burnt out.

**Hiring Multiple Editors**

Regardless of whether you or another editor is editing your writing or a combined effort, it is crucial to keep in mind the importance of the editing stages: structural editing, line and copyediting, and proofreading. Begin with big-picture editing passes and work your way down to the most specific details. Because all editors bring different skills and perspectives to the table, your best bet may be to hire a different editor to work with you on each editing process phase.

## Making a Good First Impression Through Title

According to experts, the title you choose for your book is one of the key elements that determines publication success. The book's title is crucial to the book metadata and will compose the first impression readers have of the work you have done. The title is the way your book introduces itself to the world. Your title must address a problem the reader has and provide a clear solution(s). Readers should be able to read the title and feel confident about what this book can provide to them and how it can make their life better.

Titles with explicit promises of good results are proven to engage readers. As you create your title, ask yourself what problems your book can solve for the reader, what sort of desirable skill your book will provide, or how your personal testimony and knowledge could make someone else's life better. The title should pique your reader's interest to a point where they can't wait to read more. Seek to capture the imagination of your readers, making them ponder what they might find in this book and how it could change their life. What elements of what you have to say is most fascinating, captivating, or life-changing? What kinds of emotional response do you want your story to produce in the reader? Take your time to brainstorm ideas and test out several titles until you find what works best.

## Maintaining Clarity

Your title should be simple, concise, and quickly generated to search engines to increase viewership and revenue. If you are producing a guidebook, you may use the words' how to' in the title to increase the number of hits your book will receive on the various search engines. The words you use should clearly express that you have what the potential reader needs, wants, or desires most in life. Your title should communicate what the book is about and what readers can expect to read about. Statistically, if the book is a guidebook, sales can be expected to go up if the title includes the words 'How to' by providing potential buyers with precisely what they need to know about the book.

## Catching Reader Attention

The title of your book should use catchy and creative language that make it unforgettable. Your goal is to establish a sense of character in your book and attract the readers. This attraction method may take on the form of fun, lighthearted language, humor, alliterations, or cleverness. Regardless of which way you develop this title, you should make sure it will roll off the tongue nicely, entice readers, and stick in their minds after reading it. Your title should be appropriate to the genre you are writing in and should be considerate of the target audience.

However, a romance novel's title would use much dreamier and more formal language than a horror novel title. That said, you should aim to stand out from other books in the genre.


**Keeping it Concise**

When drafting your book's title, be sure not to use any more words than you need to convey the book's theme. The shorter the title, the more likely it will show up in search engines.


Additionally, the title of the book is what will stick with readers for generations upon generations. For titles to be as memorable as possible, they should not be difficult to say or type comfortably. You should strive for a title that is easy to say in interviews and easy for people to pass between one another when recommending your book. The book title should be engaging enough to leave people feeling excited and interested, no matter how many times they have heard it. Do not make the title any longer than it needs to be. You can always expand on your description of the book using subtitles.


**Making Use of Subtitles**

If you are writing a nonfiction title specifically, it is likely you will not have enough space in the title to express what readers should expect from your book fully. In this case, subtitles can be used to increase clarity. Subtitles should be just as compelling as the title itself and should further expand on the desirable outcome described in the title. You want your title to show readers how your book can address solutions for the pain points in their lives. The subtitle is the perfect place to expand on how this will happen.

### Seeking Feedback from Your Target Audience

As you work through the process of title generation, it is important to seek feedback from your target audience. The target audience is the people you are writing to, and they are also most well-versed in other works within your genre. They can tell you what they are looking for when it comes to choosing their next book to read. The best way to do this in today's world is to join a writing group or create your own community via social media. You can utilize tools like a Facebook writing group or a social media poll for the target audience to vote from a series of title options and provide further feedback.

### Using Title Generation Tools

If you feel stuck on how to generate your title, there is no need to worry. There are endless options for title generators that can help get you started. Book title generators take what you want your title to express and apply a wide selection of names and formats to choose from. However, it is crucial to be aware of titles that fall flat. In many cases, the titles you generate on a tool should be used more as a source of inspiration than the book's actual title.

# Chapter 3: Step 3 - Intermediate Stages

As a self-publisher, your job is to publish your media in the most creative and engaging way possible. The front cover of a book is especially crucial to design. After the title, your cover is the first thing a reader can look at to consider whether or not they will begin to read the book. In this sense, cover design serves a significant purpose in communicating the message of the book. The book cover should include the author's name, the title, and any other elements or images that will intrigue the reader. The book's spine should have the title and author's name for easy identification, and the back cover should list the ISBN, author biography, and any good reader testimonies.

**Making Use of the Elements of Book Design**

The first element of book design is the front matter, which is all of the information readers will see first. This includes title pages, copyright pages, the table of contents, and forewords, prefaces, and introductions when needed. The second element is the book's body matter, which comprises the book chapters and sections. The third and final element is the back matter, which is the last parts of the book, including epilogues, appendices, and author biographies.

**Laying out Interior Book Design**

When it comes to laying out the book's interior, you have a lot of layout elements and formats at your disposal.

If you aren't sure which layout format to choose, try examining several of the books on your own bookshelf to find the fonts, layout, and trim size you like best. If you're not sure where to start, consider the following tips:

· Select a legible font and use at least 11 pt. size or larger

· Use 1.5 line spacing for easy legibility that does not use too much or too little space between sentences

· Number the pages of the book for clarity purposes

· Start chapters on the right-hand side of the page

**Designing Your Book Cover**

As previously mentioned, the front cover is an incredibly crucial element of book design. As you design your book cover or work with a designer who does, make sure to use visually appealing graphics. The cover should use imagery that elicits an emotional response and clearly communicates to the reader what they can expect. Any photos or graphics you use on the front cover should be in high resolution (you can find such images on stock photo sites, many of which are free).

Before diving into cover design, it is a good idea to explore other books' covers in your genre. What style of graphics and font are used for the title and the author's name? What elements are placed on the cover and spine, and what is their general placement? How do the graphic elements of the cover interact with the text? What can the reader glen from the book cover concerning the theme of the book? As you study the books on your own bookshelf, you can better understand the ways book covers should be designed to create a connection with the reader, inflict emotional responses, and lead them to read your book.

### Choosing a Professional Designer

Just as it is useful to invest in editors for your self-published book, it is beneficial to invest in designers. People are naturally drawn to images, and the more visually engaging your book is, the more likely readers will be to pick it up. Professional designers are trained to take a topic at hand and represent it in a visually engaging way, and they can often see things that you as the writer cannot. This is why it can be smart to invest in someone who does design for a living. Remember, there are several facets of book design. The first of these is print design, the second is ebook design, and the third is a website and digital media design. Just as it can be beneficial to invest in outside editors for your book, it can help you invest in designers.

In most cases, you cannot expect a single designer to specialize in print, ebook, and Website/digital media design, which may warrant the use of multiple designers. Before hiring a design professional, make sure you have all of the editing finished. After that piece is finished, you can often contact your local Chamber of Commerce or utilize social media to reach out to graphic designers in your area. If you want to hire a professional, there are several things to consider.

First, you should ask any candidates to provide you with a portfolio to examine the style and quality of the work they do and if they have experience with book design. Next, you will need to ask them for a price quote for design work so you can actively plan for that in your budget. After that, you will need to ask them how they handle revision requests and what general process they follow. Finally, you will need to clarify your ownership of the artwork. Feel free to ask for samples of books they have designed for other clients and clarify which program they will be using to do the design work.

**Striking a Balance in Description**

After the title and the book cover, your book description is likely the next place the reader will go to decide if they are interested in your book. The description leads readers to determine whether this book is worth their time, money, and energy. The description should include just enough information about what happens in the book to captivate the reader and make them hungry to read on. You have to strike a balance between revealing the plot's basis without providing too many details or giving away the ending. The reader should understand the basic setting and context of the story from your description, but they should not know the entire storyline.

When designing the hook sentence of your book description, you need to ask yourself what major issue is at hand in this book. What is the problem you need to solve? Use your creativity to create an engaging sentence that describes the problem that needs to be solved and makes it personal to the reader. Don't shy away from emotion in writing your description—play into it. Play into the main character's fears, suffering, or joys to spark empathy and give the reader a taste of the emotional experience they can expect in this book.

**Maintaining Third Person Point of View**

Another major thing to keep in mind in writing your book description is writing in the third person point of view. When writing a book description, you should avoid talking too much about yourself. If you do refer to yourself, for example, in a brief author byline, be sure to refer to yourself by your pronouns (he/she/they/ etc.) to maintain the third person point of view. If you include an author byline, be sure it is separated from the rest of the book as a short paragraph after the teaser for the book itself.

**Using Testimonials and Endorsements**

At the end of your book description, you should use testimonials or endorsements (as long as they enhance the description itself). Testimonials should come from someone who has read the book and had a satisfying experience or found the solution to their reading problem. You can reach out to your fanbase to submit testimonials, and even offer incentives for the best ones.

An endorsement typically comes from an authority figure who your readers are likely to recognize who has read the book and agrees that the content is beneficial, and you are qualified as an author. In many cases, celebrities, popular media sources, or other authors in the genre can be used to provide endorsements.

**Practicing Description Writing**

The last tip for writing book descriptions is to practice. Draw inspiration from the techniques used by other writers in your genre. Try highlighting different details, using different language, and experimenting with various hooks and conclusions to the description. Make a file on your computer dedicated only to the descriptions of a particular book, and feel free to share it with your network. Remember, it is normal and necessary to have multiple drafts of the same book description.

Revise it as many times as you need to feel like it perfectly describes your book. It is always a good idea to seek feedback from colleagues, mentors, or potential readers to offer their perspective. After they have looked over the description, you can ask them a series of questions to determine whether or not they truly got the message. Based on what they just read, what do they expect the book to be about?  What excites them going forward? What areas are still unclear?  Do they feel interested in reading on?  If not, what could be changed that would pique their interest? Listen carefully to other views, as their suggestions speak to the more considerable reader experience and readers' likelihood to buy your book.

# Chapter 4: Step 4 - Costs to Keep in Mind

One of the most critical steps of the self-publishing process is establishing a budget that includes all the costs and that you can stick to. The budget is ultimately up to you; some authors release ebooks as inexpensive as $1,000-$3,000, while other authors may spend much more. Regardless of where you fall on this spectrum, you must understand that all costs associated with publishing the book are your responsibility.

Within this budget, you need to think of people you may need to hire, such as professional editors and designers, as well as technical things like an ISBN, cover photos, copyright, typesetting, your own website, distribution tactics, various advertising and marketing strategies, and other miscellaneous costs. Before you begin your budgeting process, ask yourself how much money you are willing to spend and how well you want your book to sell. While it is possible to self-publish a book on a tight budget, you need to make sure you're not skimping on any details. If you let too many things slip through the cracks for the purpose of saving money, your book will be of lower quality and, therefore, less likely to sell well.

**Investing in the Editing Process**

Perhaps one of the most essential areas to budget for is the investment in a professional editor. Although it is possible to edit your book on your own, you can create a more polished version of your text if you hire a professional editor (or several) to look over your book and catch any issues with flow, context, spelling, punctuation, grammar, or general content. Even if you are a successful editor yourself, having another pair of eyes to copyedit, proofread, and check your work for consistency can make all the difference in the world.

Because the editing process has multiple stages, you may want to consider budgeting enough to pay editors who specialize in each step. In many cases, the editing stages take up the most considerable portion of costs for self-publishing. Professional editing can cost anywhere between $300-$1,500 on average. If all you need is line editing on a short book, you will probably not have to spend more than $150-$300. However, if you are in need of developmental or structural editing, you should expect to pay much more than that, depending on the length of the book. Additionally, if you choose to hire a ghostwriter, you should plan to spend more.

**Investing in Cover Design**

Another vital investment to make is in the book's cover design. In some cases, authors are talented in design and choose to design their own covers to make the project even more their own. This can be great for writers who also have particular skillsets in design, but if you are questioning your design skills at all, it's best to either hire someone or invest in a program to help you. If you want to play a part in your own cover design but don't know where to get started, you can access templates and other services on things like Amazon's Cover Creator or licensed images or templates from Canva.

If you are on a tight budget, you can access stock photography options for your cover photo (and any other images throughout the book). If you have a bit more money to dedicate to the cover, you may consider investing in a professional photo shoot to obtain your cover photo. You should also consider whether or not you want a professional headshot on your book cover, as this is an extra cost. Professional cover design typically costs between $100-$600. There are several less expensive options, such as designers who are just starting out and hoping to gain exposure or work that has already been created that you are merely paying to reuse. That said, it is vital to make sure you're not skimping on the cover design. As discussed earlier in the book, the cover is the first impression readers will receive of your book, and it is worth an investment.

### Investing in Interior Design

You also need to keep in mind the costs of your books' interior design. This is especially important if you are planning to release a print copy of the book, in which case you should plan to have your text professionally typeset. Typesetting is complex and requires a lot of skill, time, and energy, and you should prepare to make this investment in any print book. If you are releasing an eBook and are searching for customization beyond what you can find on Amazon's Kindle Create, ePub, or similar platforms, you may wish to hire a designer to help.

If you have a larger budget, you may also consider investing in a graphic designer for things like book posters, bookmarks, and business cards. It is a good idea to include general formatting costs in your design costs, ranging from $50-$300. If you're on a tight budget, you may consider looking into free or inexpensive online options for editing book interiors—just be cautious.

If you plan to sell print copies of your book, you should invest in print proofs to double-check the layouts and catch any final errors. IngramSpark can be used for paperback books, and it typically costs $30 per print proof. If you have a team of designers and editors, you will need to invest in a proof copy for each person. If you are printing your book, keep in mind that there will be fees charged by the printers.

**Investing in Online Advertisements and Websites**

While it is optional, many authors choose to invest in advertisements on social media, magazines, or TV to increase publicity and sales. Some companies assist with marketing and media exposure for a fee. In many cases, authors choose to create a website in which to promote themselves and build a community among their target audience. Your website can serve as an author platform through which to write blogs, expand your business, and gain publicity for your works.

Whether you choose a paid website developer or choose to use a free one like WordPress or Blogger, there are several costs you should be prepared to be responsible for. The first of these is website hosting, which generally costs around $150 per year. You may also need to purchase a domain name, especially if you want to increase the number of people who find your website. The cost for a domain name is relatively low, at around $10-$15 annually.

Lastly, if you want to collect email addresses to compile a mailing list, you will need to pay for an email subscription service. This service will manage all of your emails. In many cases, you can find an email subscription service for as low as $10 per month, depending on how many subscribers you have. If you are hoping to run ads on your website, you should set aside a budget of between $100-$500.

## Making Technical Investments

In terms of more technical self-publishing investments, you should be prepared to invest in an ISBN. The ISBN is a unique code that will allow bookstores and libraries to access the book's necessary information quickly. While there are free options that exist (such as CreateSpace and IngramSpark), your book is less likely to be carried in bookstores if you don't invest any money in it. Free ISBNs cause further limitations in that they prohibit eBooks from being stocked on Overdrive, which is a website that circulates eBooks to public libraries worldwide. The cost of getting an ISBN is $295 for 10 ISBN codes, which is worth it when you consider all of the channels of distribution it will open up for you.

## Determining Miscellaneous Budget Items

There are several final miscellaneous items to include in your budget. The first of these is the cost to register your manuscript with the Library of Congress and get it copyrighted. You should plan for events such as book signings or release parties and the costs associated with those. Additionally, you should save room in your budget for random logistical items such as shipping, packaging, office supplies, and bookstands. You may also choose to have your book made into an audiobook, which is generally an added cost of between $300-$3,000 (again depending on the length of the book). It is a good idea to have a specific portion of your budget set aside for the miscellaneous items, so you can be prepared to foot unexpected costs if they arise

### Budget Planning in Three Categories

As you begin to plan your budget, it's best to divide the process into three categories. First, you should determine what you can comfortably accomplish yourself (while making sure they are still professional and that you can be free of errors). Second, you should evaluate the things you need to pay someone else to do and where you plan to look for those people to hire. Lastly, ask yourself what items you may be able to barter for with friends.

If you have a friend who is a graphic designer, for example, they may be able to help you with your cover or interior design for a discounted price. If you have a friend who works as an editor, you may be able to share your skills with them in exchange for them to do an editing pass on your book. No matter how you choose to divide the three categories in your budgeting process, you need to make sure you have generated an all-encompassing total cost. Once you have determined this total cost, you can determine how many copies of your book you'll need to sell to break even and how many you would need to sell to profit.

# Chapter 5: Step 5 - Marketing and Distribution

When it comes to self-publishing, marketing is one of the greatest keys to success. Before you even begin to write your book, you should begin marketing. You should be able to identify the *why,* that is, the reason you are choosing to write this book. You should then identify the *what,* which describes what impact you hope the book will have and what your readers have to gain from it. As previously described, you should be sure to determine who your market is, what they want, and how your book can satisfy that need and create the impact you desire. Once you have answered these key questions, you will have a greater sense of direction in your marketing strategy.

**Developing your Marketing Campaign**

When you approach the book marketing process, you should do so as you would approach any other businesses. Marketing campaigns take a great deal of skill and attention to detail to accurately portray your audience's gain from your book. How can you help the people who will read your book? How will their life be better after reading it? Once you have answered these questions, you will have a direction for communicating with your readers and making it clear to them why they should read your book.

## Investing in Communication

As a self-publisher, you should invest in communication with your readers. This communication can take on many forms. Some self-publishers choose to spend hours researching within their niche and reading others' work, so they know the best and most current tips and tricks to use. Other self-publishers invest time in learning strategies of online traffic keywords to direct more attention to their works. Some spend a great deal of time investing in their social media and generating a following through which to gain readers. Some may opt for a more traditional method of placing their book in physical spaces, such as libraries, bookstores, or other stores and having tables at conventions and other events.

## Marketing Using Book Reviews

In many cases, you can use book reviews as a way to market your book. Book reviews use persuasive language and are editorial, not promotional, which makes them appear more genuine. Honest reviews of your book help it be seen for what it is and make it clear to your audience what they are getting into. You can also use author platforms, such as a personal website and your social media accounts. In today's world, online marketing is often more effective and less expensive than traditional strategies.

## Implementing a Planning Process

One of the most critical aspects of marketing is the planning process. The most effective planning process has several, which are as follows: segment your markets, target your best customers, understand how, when, and where your customers buy books, and what motivates them to do so, and create a position through which to bring in targeted customers.

## Determining Top Markets

When it comes to segmenting your customers, you must remember that it is impossible to check every reader's box. It is essential to understand how different people may choose to use your book and those who are most likely to make frequent investments for their purposes.

You will likely come up with a long list of potential buyers, and you should know that it is impossible to market to all of them equally. From the list, you should come up with your top markets, which will create your targets. Developing your target groups does not mean you are ignoring individuals who are not in those groups; it merely means they are not your focus.

**Marketing to the Needs of the Target Audience**

As your buyers decide which books to buy, they have a number of things they are looking for. If you are writing a book that targets college-aged voters, you may find that your book would do best in an election year, as tensions are high, and voting is a topic of higher focus. Your target audience may be motivated to buy your book if they know it can tell them what they need to know to form their opinions on voting and have their questions answered.

Your position, then, would be the way you use the topic that motivates your target audience. In this case, you may adopt a position of addressing the fact that college-aged voters may feel intimidated by voting and have questions they are afraid to ask. You can approach them from a place of non-judgment that will help them get all the answers they need to be informed voters in the upcoming election.

**Understanding the Buying Process**

When it comes to marketing, you should also understand the stages of the buying process. The buying process has five steps: problem recognition, informative search, alternative evaluation, purchase decision, and post-purchase evaluation. Understanding this model is crucial if you want to sell your book.

## Problem Recognition

The first step of the process, problem recognition, happens when a buyer realizes they have a problem. In your college-aged voter target audience, the problem is that they feel intimidated about voting and are full of questions they don't know how to get answered. In order to sell your book to them, you must prove why the information within it provides a solution to this problem by answering their questions and equipping them with useful information about voting, so they feel more confident.

You must be aware of the fact that problems vary greatly depending on the market you are working within and the population of your target audience. Nonfiction books, like the one about voting, are geared towards educating the reader and being informative to obtain the desired solution. Fiction books, however, are more focused on solving entertainment-related problems.

## Evaluating Alternatives

Once a buyer has discovered they have a problem, they will start looking for a way to solve that problem. This leads to the second stage of the process, which is evaluating alternatives. In this stage, the buyer is thinking of various ways to solve their problem, and they likely will be trying to choose between several books to get the solutions. In this case, it can be helpful to provide free samples of your writing that will give the reader a taste and further implore them to purchase your book.

## Making the Right Choice

After they have evaluated alternatives, they will move into a phase of deciding whether or not to make the purchase. At this point, the buyer will be worried about making the right choice. This is an opportunity to follow up with them and encourage them towards the purchase by explaining how it will be worth it and improving their lives. It is imperative not to lose connection with potential buyers during this stage. Overall, you must have a good understanding of your customer's buying processes to plan out your timing.

## Adhering to the Buyer's Timeline

Be prepared that customers will all function at slightly different timings, and you should seek to adhere to their schedules. That said, you should be ready to intercept multiple customers at multiple times and in numerous contexts. You may use your website or social media accounts to have giveaways, question and answer sessions, or teasers to keep your readers engaged and promote your work.

## Mastering Online Distribution

Equally important to marketing your book in the world, is distributing it. From the time you begin to tell potential buyers about your book, you should be thinking of the most effective ways to get it into their hands. In today's world of technology, you should know that more than half of all book sales (both print and eBooks) take place online. This is crucial knowledge for the self-publisher when it comes to distribution, and it can be used to your advantage in that you have the same, inexpensive access to the online world as any major publishers do. When it comes to book retailers, Amazon is ranked highest globally, no matter the format of the books being sold.

One way to get your book circling online is by creating direct relationships with online retailers. If you are in communication with these online retailers, you will have more control and access to marketing and promotion tools. If you work with eBook distribution services, you will likely have to give up a certain percentage of your profits. However, many of these distributors have access to exclusive promotion and marketing tools, which may help you reach a wider audience and sell more copies.

### Determining Print Distribution Options

In terms of distributing print books, print-on-demand options are typically best for new self-publishers. Print-on-demand means that your book will not be printed until after someone has ordered and paid for it. Each order constitutes one printed book, which will then be shipped out to the paying customer. Printing on demand reduces the risk of spending too much money on printing and having many books leftover. That said, it also reduces the likelihood that your book will be sitting on the shelves of popular retailers. It is essential to look at your budget and weigh out the pros and cons when deciding how to distribute your print book.

### Making Use of Aggregators

Whether you are planning to distribute digitally or in print, you will want to know how to use an aggregator. Aggregators are companies that allow you to upload your books to a single place, from which they will be distributed to other platforms. Several popular aggregators are Smashwords, IngramSpark, PublishDrive, and Draft2Digital.Out of these, IngramSpark is the one that allows for single uploads for both eBook and print. Most other aggregators require separate uploads to be made. You can use a variety of distributors in combination with other another or separately.

There is no set answer for how many aggregators to make use of at one time. If you have the time and energy, it's a good idea to spread yourself across various individual platforms. When you do this, your royalties will go up, and you may have increased access to things like promotions.

## Choosing a Distributor

When it comes to what to look for in a distributor, there are several factors to consider. The first thing you should do is compare the reputations of various distributors. What are other authors saying about this distributor? If the reviews you find are mostly negative or have trouble locating reviews in general, it's best to steer clear. To that same token, you must take into account the reliability of the distributor. Is their service known for reliable content delivery to readers? After you have determined this, you should assess the ease of use of a particular distributor. You want the service(s) you choose to be as quick and painless as possible in terms of digital file publishing and distribution. Lastly, you should examine your budget and compare the cost-effectiveness of various distributors. Make sure to look at every detail of cost involved so you can identify the actual price and compare which distributors are the best value for the money.

# Chapter 6: Step 6 - Self-Publishing Mistakes to Avoid

Like in every industry, there are numerous mistakes in the self-publishing field that you should be aware of and take action to avoid. The self-publishing industry is becoming more extensive and more competitive by the day, and therefore, it is more important than ever to be diligent in preventing mistakes.

**Being Lazy with Editing**

One of the first significant mistakes you can make in self-publishing is to be lazy with the editing process. Grammar and spelling errors, inconsistencies, and clichés may seem insignificant at times, but in reality, these things pose massive stumbling blocks to the reader. Books that are poorly edited are challenging to get through and do not gain the same respect in the industry as their well-edited counterparts.

While there are self-publishers who edit their own work, you have to be meticulous and conduct far more editing passes (with sufficient breaks in between) than you may think necessary. Better still is to edit the book a time or two yourself, then hire a professional editor or editing team for each of the types of editing. Before sending your book out into the world, you must make sure that it has undergone enough editing passes to have every stage of the process completed.

## Formatting Incorrectly

Along the same lines as editing, another fatal flaw of a self-publisher is incorrectly formatting the book. It is crucial to make yourself aware of the various stipulations booksellers have in place and abide by those standards in your formatting process. Be sure to thoroughly read the guidelines and note the required file types, graphic formatting, and general manuscript formatting requirements (such as line spacing, paragraphs, and section breaks).

## Failing to Reach Out

Not only do some authors fail to have proper editing and formatting, but they also fail to open up the book to trusted members of the target audience to provide feedback. If no one reads your book before it is published, you will send it out into the world with no idea of what your readers will enjoy or the places it still needs work. Friends, family members, and trusted audience members can provide honest feedback and shed light on areas you may not have previously noticed. Better yet is to join a writing community that provides both support and necessary criticism. Not being willing to accept criticism is one major flaw of many self-publishers, and it can truly impact the overall success of that book.

**Slacking on Cover Design**

Another major self-publishing mistake is making the minimal effort on your cover design. As mentioned previously, the cover of your book is the first impression—it sets a precedent for the rest of the book and helps readers decide whether they are initially interested or not. In an attempt to save money, many authors choose to create their own front covers with minimal design experience. The authors who do this probably assume that the rest of their book will be enough to capture the reader's attention, and therefore, that it's okay to have an average cover.

The problem with this is that if the cover is unappealing, the reader will not even bother to look over other book elements. If you can't hook them with the cover, you have almost no hope of getting them to the next step of the decision process; they will simply rule out your book without a second thought. Therefore, unless you are skilled in design and publishing techniques, the decision to skimp on the cover of your book could completely tank your sales.

**Writing a Poor Book Description**

Earlier in the chapter, we discussed the importance of a good book description. After the cover, your book description is the next impression of the book as a whole, and you have to make it count. A crucial mistake many self-publishers make is to be boring, rambling, or self-righteous in their description. If readers feel disengaged, lost, or condescended, it is an immediate turn-off from reading the rest of the book. To avoid making this mistake, you should make an effort to read as many example descriptions from your genre as possible. What are the typical structures authors use? What plot points are highlighted? The more familiar you are with these strategies, the more likely you are to engage your reader and set a helpful precedent for the rest of the book.

**Losing Sight of the Market**

Another common mistake self-publishers make is not taking the time to analyze the market. The best self-publishers know what types of books are selling and why, and they know how to play into those statistics. Not taking the time to conduct thorough research on the market, potential competition, and your demographic can be a crucial mistake. To that same token, not marketing at all is another fatal flaw of many self-publishers. If people haven't heard of their book, they will have no reason to buy it.

As a self-publisher, you must be able to talk about yourself and the work that you do, even before it is published. In a world of ever-growing technology, you will not be able to reach your full potential unless you fully take advantage of marketing via social media. Use things like polls, questions and answers, and teasers to keep your readers and fans engaged with the writing process from start to finish, ultimately giving them no choice but to buy the book when it is released. Identify your personal network of friends, family, followers, and your writing community, rely on them to help you with promotion and buy their book for themselves or gift to other people in their lives. Do not be afraid to ask your support system to promote you.

**Releasing Books at the Wrong Time**

When it comes to releasing books into the world, timing is crucial. Lousy timing can destroy your book's potential for success completely. Pay attention to the calendar. What season are you releasing your book in? How do members of your audience often react to that season? What is the political and cultural climate? What are the significant events of the day? What are people talking about? All of these are crucial considerations when it comes to the timing of releasing your book. How can the release of your book correspond with what is happening in the world?

**Losing Track of Your Release Date**

Another major mistake self-publishers make is failing to select and stick to a particular release date in terms of timing. Throughout the marketing process, you must be able to cultivate audience expectations and set the tone of yourself as a reliable person. When arranging your release date, be realistic. Don't push yourself to deadlines you may not be able to reach—give yourself more time than you need to leave room for things to go wrong. If you give yourself this leeway, you can avoid letting your audience down.

### Selling your Book for the Wrong Price

When you go to sell your book, another major mistake to look out for is trying to sell it for the wrong price. If the price is too high, people will not only not buy your book but also respect it less. If it is too low, your sales may increase, but you will not be profiting in the way you deserve. Additionally, if a book is priced too low, readers may draw conclusions about the book's quality and assume that it's too cheap to be worth the read. The best way to avoid mispricing your book is to research other books' average prices within your genre. Additionally, it's a good idea to analyze how other authors use promotional discounts and be smart with your personal use to increase your sales.

### Limiting Distribution Channels

In an earlier chapter, we discussed the variety of channels through which to distribute your book. While it can be possible to achieve success using only one distributor, this can also be a mistake. In many cases, self-publishers restrict themselves and the book's potential success by using only one channel. To avoid this, allow yourself to use as many distributors as physically possible. What do you have to lose?

**Losing Faith in the Face of Failure**

The final major mistake self-publishers make to quit if the first book doesn't do well. This is a cutthroat industry, and persistence is absolutely crucial if you want to "make it" as an author. To keep your spirits up, you should view each book you write as an experience from which to grow, no matter the outcome. Each failure is fuel for future success, and you must be patient and persistent. The worst mistake you can make is to give up too soon. Don't rush yourself— take all the necessary actions and then allow things to happen in their time. By doing things right the first time, you can increase your chances for success once the book is out in the world.

When you have finished writing your first book, allow yourself to celebrate what you have accomplished. Writing a book is a massive accomplishment in itself, and one you should be proud of yourself for achieving. With every book you write, you have the chance to develop your fan base, change your strategy, and continue to increase your popularity. Although this chapter has been focused on the mistakes to avoid, it is also important to remember that mistakes are part of the growth process. With each book you write and mistake you commit; you have a chance to try something new the next time.

# Chapter 7: Step 7 - Tips for Successful Self-Publishers

In the previous chapter, we discussed the significant mistakes for self-publishers to avoid. This chapter will seek to engage in reframing mistakes to avoid into secrets to apply to your writing process. Throughout this chapter, we will discuss several tips to unlock your most profound potential as a self-publisher, and truly set yourself apart from others.

**Taking it Step by Step**

The first tip for successful self-publishers goes hand in hand with the mistakes to avoid. As previously mentioned, cutting corners in editing, design, or marketing can abolish a book's potential for success. If your book is sloppily edited, you will lose reader's attention, respect, and level of enjoyment in reading. If you slack on design, your book will be easily overlooked on the shelves, and readers will be discouraged from taking even the first step in engaging with your text. If you are closeminded in your marketing strategies, or worse yet, don't engage in marketing at all, you will have done all of that work only to sell very few copies.

Ultimately, if you choose to go on the journey of self-publishing, go there fully, without cutting corners. By choosing to be thorough in every single part of the process, checking, double-checking, and reaching out for professional help and outsider perspective, your book has the potential to go from good to extraordinary. While it is important to keep costs in mind, you will need to be careful not to sell yourself short. When you set out to self-publish a book, you should set out with the decision to invest in the parts of the process that will enhance your level of success.

## Finding Your Niche

The next tip is to be acutely aware of your niche and what kind of content you want to write within that niche. Every human being has particular gifts and passions and a unique life story and way of seeing the world. Perhaps you are a naturally sensitive, hopeless romantic who sees the beauty in nearly every person and place you encounter. Knowing this about yourself, you would likely determine that the place for you is within the niche of romance novel writing. After you have determined that, ask yourself what parts of your perception on romance could make for an interesting story. Locate the gaps that exist in the niche, and ask yourself how you can fill them.

After you have taken time to analyze all of your contributions, passions, interest areas, and experiences, narrow it down to the niche where you have the most to say and will be most well-received. Be sure to keep the context in mind—what element of your story or perspective is most applicable to your target audience? What is the target audience most in need of from your content? Why does the world need this book, and what qualifies you to be the one to write it? Once you have answered these questions, you can effectively narrow down your options to identify your content's best potential niche(s). You can use your target audience's needs to guide your writing process and marketing strategies and cultivate your fanbase and potential for future successes.

### Establishing Realistic Goals

Before you begin writing, you should be aware of your personal goals. Why have you decided to set out on this journey? Knowing your purpose and what you hope to provide and gain through the self-publishing experience can more accurately shape your process. Having a clear picture in your head allows you to set realistic goals for your needs and what you hope to achieve. Let's say that one of your goals is to sell a high number of books. You must look at your experience and define "a lot of books" accordingly.

If you are new at self-publishing and have not yet had the chance to establish an audience, you should start a relatively low number and work your way up. Establish a plan for how to expand your author platform, build a fanbase, and market yourself so that your sales can regularly progress. Take time to develop a thorough business plan with daily action steps. What will you do every day to remain consistent with your goals? Take several sticky notes and write your goals on them, then paste them all over your workspace so you can constantly remind yourself the reason for starting this journey, and motivate yourself to stay on it.

## Relationship Building and Collaboration

Earlier in the book, we discussed the importance of building your team and trading off skills with friends, professionals, fans, and a writing community. Collaborative relationships open the doors for you to try new things, gain new perspectives and chances for exposure, and cultivate new strategies for success. It is crucial to know who your network is and tap into that. How can your story grow stronger by playing off the insight of your community? Where is your target audience showing up, and how can you meet them there?

In addition to the relationships mentioned, it is also useful to collaborate with outside organizations, non-profits, and community events. You can collaborate with schools, libraries, local bookstores, etc. for book tours, signings, and other events to boost your exposure. You should dedicate plenty of time to researching what's happening with your community, and drafting pitches to various organizations about why the promotion of your book can benefit their organization.

## Always Keep Writing

The final tip for self-publishing success is to keep writing, even if you're hitting a wall or feel like the book is finished. Don't let your writing go stagnant—challenge yourself to write a little bit every day, implementing different prompts and techniques. You can keep up with writing by using daily journals, writing entries on your author blog, writing monthly newspaper or magazine columns, or simply sitting down with a pen and paper for a brainstorming session. By continuing to write, you can develop your professional skills and continue to get the word out about the books you've written and the role you play as an author in your niche. Continue to add to your portfolio, book as many events as possible, and remain in a constant state of seeking new opportunities to grow your author platform.

**Making a Daily Commitment**

When you choose to embark on the self-publishing journey, you must understand that you are making a daily commitment. As a self-published author, you must commit to waking up every day with something new to learn, plan, or complete. You must create a life around who you are as an author and learn to find opportunities for success in every corner of the world. You should view the world as your toolbox, taking inspiration from the people and events around you, as well as the passions, skills, and interests you have been gifted with.

# Conclusion

You picked up this guide with the understanding that the self-publishing route was the route you wanted to go and the desire to dive into the logistics of the journey. You likely began this guide with an understanding of the industry's cutthroat nature and the preparedness to learn the details of every part of the process. You understood that in order to be successful, you had to familiarize yourself with the mistakes other self-publishers have made, as well as their secrets to rising to the top of the industry. You had an awareness of all that is at stake in the self-publishing process, especially as it pertains to setting yourself apart from other writers within your genre.

At the start of this guide, you were introduced to the things that set self-publishing apart from publishing with a company. You learned that you have more agency through self-publishing and can call all the shots on marketing, design, and showcasing your creativity. You are in charge of every element of your book, from the beginning of the process to the end, and you can operate freely from publishing companies. When you become a successful self-publisher, there is truly nothing that can stand in your way on your journey to the top.

Throughout the guide, you were provided with the ins and outs of the self-publishing process, from the beginning stages of writing, editing, and generating a title, to the intermediate stages of book design and description writing, to the details of budgeting, marketing, and distribution. You learned the importance of reaching out to other people on a personal and professional level to guide you and make sure you are staying on track with your intentions and appeals to the target audience.

You learned what mistakes to avoid to be as successful as possible, as well as the secret tips of the most successful self-publishers. You learned how to establish yourself as a reliable and well-respected author who regularly engages with their fanbase and keeps the fans involved in the process. You learned how to make your own process and use your creativity, voice, and marketing strategies to your advantage, as well as tips for how and where to distribute.

You discovered the importance of being thorough throughout every step of the process, as well as the benefits of reaching out for help from professional editors and designers. You learned the importance hearing from the target audience members to ask for advice and perspective. You learned that in order to distinguish yourself as a self-published author, you must identify the gaps that exist in your genre and decide how you can fill them. You also discovered the benefits of breaking each stage down into a multi-step process to keep yourself and your team on track.

Throughout the course of this guide, you have learned every skill you need to become a successful self-publisher. With this guide by your side as your trusty self-publishing guide, nothing can steer you wrong!

# Book 2: How to Write Fiction

*7 Easy Steps to Master Fiction Writing, Novel Writing,*

*Writing a Book & Short Story Writing*

Jaiden Pemton

# Introduction

There is a magic in storytelling that has been present and passed down from generation to generation. When it comes to writing fiction, you have the entire world at your fingertips, and you can create anything you desire. Fiction allows us to take elements of our knowledge, experience, and passions, and mold a reality for our own. As fascinating as this is, the task itself can be incredibly daunting. If you find your characters falling flat, your setting getting lost in the background, your point of view changes throughout the story, or your theme becoming lost in the chaos, you are not alone. When it comes to writing fiction, there are a lot of things to keep in mind in order to keep the reader engaged and be sure the story is being told in a way that is memorable, meaningful, and easy to follow.

While it can be difficult to discern the best way to channel story ideas into a cohesive fiction piece, the process of fiction writing doesn't have to be as overwhelming and chaotic as it may seem at first glance. All it takes is a deeper understanding of each of the elements of fiction writing. Also, the details that influence how each of those elements unfolds. This guide breaks down the details within each step of fiction writing, opens your mind to new possibilities, and helps you to come in touch with your goals for fiction writing.

The chapters of this guide will take you through each step of fiction-writing in a way that will help you check all the boxes and avoid common mistakes. Each detail is designed to keep you on track and answer any and all questions you may have about fiction writing. These sections contain all the information you need to develop well-rounded characters, a logical plot, an in-depth and meaningful setting, a suitable point of view, and a relevant and influential theme for each fiction story you write. Throughout the journey, you will find yourself discovering your own writing voice, and experimenting with

various styles of fiction writing until you find the one that is the best fit for you.

Each chapter is organized in an easy-to-follow, subtitled format with comprehensive examples of every tip, trick, and technique. This all-inclusive guide to fiction writing also contains a number of special fiction-writing secrets embedded throughout the text, which can help to develop your skills as a writer further. Whether you are aiming to write fiction stories based upon experiences in this world or another, this guide has all the tools you need and is sure to serve as the perfect guide to revolutionize your fiction writing experience.

Happy writing!

# Chapter 1: Step 1 - Building Characters

Before you can begin to tell a story, you must determine who the people are that are enduring the story. It is the characters who make the story move—who draw the reader into a new world and make them feel a part of it. The most important part of character development is to make your characters feel entirely real. If the character seems flat, aloof, or unrelatable, your reader will not be able to create a connection with them, and they will entirely lose interest in the rest of the story. Therefore, developing real, raw, and complex characters should be in the forefront of your character developing process. Think back to when you were a child. If you ever walked away from a movie or finished a book and found yourself imagining what your life would be like as the characters, that means the characters were well-developed. Something about the way those characters were represented, even if they lived in a society, era, or lifestyle that was entirely different than your own, made you feel like you could put yourself in their shoes.

Additionally, real and raw characters are more likely to portray the deeper messages of the book because the reader will develop a sense of trust and compatibility with them.

**Character Introduction**

It is vital to introduce your character to the reader at the beginning of the story so they may begin to develop a strong initial connection. Certain hard and fast details like age, cultural background, nationality, voice, occupation, and markable physical qualities like tattoos, style of dress, beauty marks, or imperfections are important to establish an initial image in the reader's mind. Another way to set characters apart and create individual images for each of them is to give them a tag. Tags are notable qualities such as an accent, a particular piece of jewelry, a unique gesture or mannerism, or a passion unique to that character. If, for example, your protagonist is in love with a girl down the street who has black and white tattoos all the way up her arms, this is not only an initial point of interest but also a distinguishing element of that character to make them stick in the reader's mind and bring back throughout the story. Additionally, the significance of the girl's tattoos can lead to opportunities for dialogue between characters and a deeper representation of the girl's personality and life.

From the beginning, your reader should have enough details to have a distinguished image and voice in their head whenever a particular character enters the scene. Once you have introduced your characters, it is important to establish trust with your reader, giving them credit to use their own imaginations and develop a unique understanding of each character as they read the story. One of the most important elements of fiction writing is "show, don't tell." You should not have to provide a lengthy narrative summary to develop your reader's understanding of the characters. Rather, the character's background story, daily choices, internal dialogue, and the way they orient themselves in the world should speak for themselves.

**Establishing Character Depth**

After the initial introduction, your characters will continue to unfold into three-dimensional figures. Remember that character development involves creating an entire human being with a past, a present, and a future—you must be thorough. Although you may not reveal every single element of your character's past in the story itself, you must personally be aware of every single detail that composes that character and their experience. Basic descriptions of physical qualities and personality traits are not enough to establish depth. Take a piece of paper, and write out the elements of your character's life from their birth until the present moment. Where were they born? Who are their parents? What did their family unit (or lack thereof) look like? What sort of impact has this had on their development? What is the relationship status of this character? Do they work or attend school? Do they have any children? Who are the people in this character's circle; do they have a best friend? What are this character's hopes, dreams, skills, and talents? What most commonly produces an issue in their everyday life or stands in their way?

You should establish a personal awareness of what triggers anger, fear, grief, or trauma in this character, and why that is so. It is also important to assign a personality type to your character. Is this character a peacemaker who sometimes struggles to put their own needs first, or are they constantly ready to speak up, challenge authority, and fight until they are heard? Perhaps this character is a deep creative who feels largely misunderstood by the world, or a timid, rule-abiding personality trying desperately to find their own voice.

**Making Characters Relatable**

It is impossible to identify or empathize with any character who does not possess human qualities. This means you must have a basic understanding of human psychology, how people's brains work, and what causes people to react to things the way they do. If, for example, your character possesses superhuman strength, is kind at all times and never runs out of patience or energy, has no physical flaws, or never experiences emotional conflicts, your reader will not feel that they can relate. Humans are imperfect and flawed, and conflict is a regular aspect of our lives. It is important to keep this fact in mind when you approach fiction writing.

Your character should have flaws, just as every human being does. However, because your main character must possess some heroic qualities, you must ensure that these flaws are forgivable, identifiable, and easy to empathize with. It is important to dedicate plenty of time to define your character's flaws, how these flaws impact their lives, and how they move beyond (and in spite of) them. Your character will struggle, but they should never be portrayed as weak or cowardly. Although they have flaws, there should always be heroic qualities present that keep your reader engaged and rooting for character growth and success.

**Growth as Expressed by the Character Arc**

In terms of growth, it is vital to understand the "character arc". The character arc represents the path on which a character grows and changes throughout the story. Just as human beings are constantly changing as a result of what we learn and experience, so it should be for fictional characters. Throughout the story, great attention should be given to the character's inner dialogue. What keeps your character awake at night? Do they have any secrets? What is their largest fear, shame, and driving force? At the end of the story, what does your character know about themselves or the world that they did not know before? How has their life changed as a result of what has happened to them? How have they grown as a person? How do they approach the future?

In the book *The Alchemist,* for example, the young shepherd boy begins the book striving for something greater but feeling unsure of how to get there. Throughout the course of his journey to find the treasure, he is met with insights on his interactions with other people, the fire at the heart of every human being that can act as a guiding force, and the presence of omens to guide people towards that life purpose. His character develops until he has made the pinnacle observation of where to find the truths of life and oneself.

### Making it Personal

When it comes to fictional character development, it can be helpful to take personal inspiration. Consider the complexities of your own life, personality, and those of the people you know. You can take the approach of changing several details of a personal experience to create a new circumstance. What are some ways that particular circumstance could have turned out? How do you wish it went? Could it have gone worse? In fiction, you have the freedom to base your characters off of real people in real experiences, while changing as many details as necessary to create your own story. We will take more about personification in later chapters.

### Writing Exercise: Putting Yourself in Their Shoes

One of the greatest joys of writing fiction is the freedom to embody the characters you create. Whatever you dream of being—the villain, the heroine, someone of a different personal or cultural background, a mystical creature, a young child, a single mother, a soldier—fiction gives you the space to be that person. Every time you sit down to write on a certain character, take a few moments to close your eyes, breathe deeply, and truly become that character. At every twist and turn of the story, ask yourself, "what would I do if I were in this character's shoes right now?"

As you develop your characters, ask yourself which words you can use to summarize that character's personality most accurately. Are they bold and confrontational or shy and reserved? If the character is bold and aggressive, you may write about circumstances in which they stand up for the ones they love and fight for the underdog when no one else will. However, their confrontational nature may also get them into trouble when they grow passionate and have trouble controlling their abrupt reactions. Putting yourself in your character's shoes can guide the events of the story, as well as the character's growth. In the case of the bold and confrontational character, perhaps they feel that in order to be strong, they must not be soft in any way. Over the course of the story, their character arc may involve learning about the strength that lies in being soft and allowing their guard to come down sometimes. In the case of the shy and reserved character, their journey may involve learning the strength in their own voice and how to use it to influence change.

**Establishing Character Credibility**

A final important detail of character development is establishing credibility. Although fiction writing gives you the freedom to make your characters whoever you want them to be, you will not be able to develop them without some research fully. If you are writing a character who comes from a different personal or cultural background than your own, has a different passion or occupation than your own, or has experienced a tragedy that you have not. It is not enough to base their story off of simply what you imagine it might be like. To create a well-rounded character for your readers to fully understand and empathize with, you must literally put yourself in that character's shoes. One way to do this is by finding interviewees who have had similar experiences to your character and can answer questions to generate a deeper understanding. If you are writing on an ER nurse, for example, you could try calling into a local hospital and asking for an ER nurse who would be willing to book an interview about a day in their life. Begin by asking the interviewee to describe a typical day in their life, doing the things the character in your book will be doing. Develop several questions to serve as a guide, then follow up with further questions as the interview goes. Be prepared to be surprised and confront ideas you were not prepared for. All of those details are important to include in order to establish true character credibility.

Another great option is to go into an environment like that of which your character lives or works in. In the case of the ER nurse, you may want to try to schedule a day to go into that environment and shadow an ER nurse on their day at work. Take field notes of everything you observe. You may even find that you can draw further inspiration from the specific details of that setting and the people you see there. You can go into any neighborhood, classroom, landscape, or other environments with a journal and allow it to move you freely. Write down your observations and any feelings you experience in that setting, and channel them into the description of your characters and their lives.

# Chapter 2: Step 2 - Shaping the Story Through Plot Development

As you take on the beginning steps of fiction writing, you will often find that plot development and character development happen subsequently at times. The plot feeds heavily off of the characters navigating through it. And how they develop from the start of the story to the end. When planning out the specifics of what happens in your story, there are several key questions to ask yourself. First of all, you should identify a primary sequence of events and how your characters change over time as a result of those events. What locations does each of these events happen in? How does each of these events contribute to the larger structure of the story? How does it do with the development of its characters?

**The Importance of the 5 W's (Who, What, When, Where, Why)**

The 5 W's are one of the most important clarifying factors of any story. You should establish straight away who the important characters are, where the story is unfolding when the story is unfolding, what situation the characters are in, and why they ended up there. The best stories are not only clear about each of these 5 W's; they also provide room for circumstances to change. You can further engage your reader by demonstrating changes in the who as your protagonist finds a new part of themselves and unlocks new strength. Another example of engaging your reader in the who of your plot is if one of the characters turns out to have an identity. They have been hiding that is revealed later on in the story. This may bring an element of surprise to the reader and cause them to shift their perspective. Perhaps the where may change as the protagonist gets a new job or moves to a new city. You can also change the what by detailing revelations your character has about what their true goal in life is. Take as much time as you need to generate thorough answers to these questions.

## Plot Development Toolbox: Outlines, Timelines, and Storyboards

In the beginning stages, you may find it helpful to create an outline that provides a detailed summary of how the book flows and how each event is connected. It can also be helpful to create a comprehensive timeline of events in the novel, which can later branch off into separate chapters. Storyboards are an excellent tool to keep you on track as you move through each of the story's scenes. On note cards, post-it notes, or something similar, you can detail which of your characters will be involved in each scene, and what the main point of that particular scene is. You will then have the opportunity to reorder the scenes as the story develops until you end up with the most logical sequence. As you transition from the planning process to the actual writing, you should be able to describe what the story is about using only two sentences. Once you can do this, you know that your ideas are fully developed, and the story has a strong foundation on which to be built.

## Plot Introduction (What's the Main Goal?)

As you begin to introduce your characters at the beginning of the story, you must also introduce the plot by making the reader aware of each character's main goals. Be specific in describing these goals. For example, it is not sufficient to say that your protagonist wants to be a writer in the future. What kind of writing does she want to do? Does she hope to live in a certain area? How do her dreams impact the way she envisions herself in the future? It is far better to say that she wants to be a famous poet, living alone in a mountain cottage, and traveling the world, than simply that she wants to be a writer. The main goal should be established as a driving force to the character's life—it is the most important thing to them. This goal will shape why the character chooses to act the way they do. What decisions do they make? How does their goal motivate them and define their daily life?

Be sure that any main goals you present are realistic and attainable. Remember, you want your characters to be established as human beings first and foremost so that the reader can relate to them and empathize with them. Leave room for the story to continue developing and for the main goal to expand and change after the protagonist is faced with conflict. Large-scale plot development should be fueled by the basic, everyday moments the characters experience. You can reveal a lot about the underlying themes of the story by giving small details such as how a character engages in dialogue or what sorts of simple actions they take (such as how they make their commute in the mornings or how they decorate their desk).

**Exposition**

This crucial introduction to the characters and their motivations occurs in the exposition. The exposition is the first part of plot development, in which characters are introduced within an established setting. There should be some explanation of the primary themes and main events of the story. The central conflict should be evident from the beginning, and it should draw the reader in and make them want to know what happens next. The exposition will introduce whether the structure of the story is linear or non-linear. Linear structure is chronological—it starts at the beginning and builds from there. Non-linear structure, however, drops a reader into a moment right in the middle of things. This gives the reader a chance to understand the central conflict in terms of what is going on. But not why it is happening. If the story opens with a woman next to her unconscious boyfriend at a hospital, the reader comes to know both characters and that they are in the hospital. But the readers do not understand how they got there. Non-linear structures can create added tension by introducing effects before causes, and this approach can be very engaging for readers, making them hungry for answers.

For the purpose of exploring these elements of plot, let's consider the classic story *The Three Little Pigs.* In this story, the exposition of the plot is when all three pigs are introduced in the setting of the countryside. It is clear in the beginning that each pig has one goal in mind: to build their own house. From the beginning, we know that one pig is building their house of straw, one is using sticks, and the third is taking their time to build a sturdy house of bricks. We are introduced to the main goals and potential themes from the very beginning when we see how the pigs who use straw and sticks are in a hurry to finish building so they can just have fun. The pig who uses bricks, however, is patient and takes the necessary time to develop a sturdy house that can endure much more. Due to its rudimentary nature as a children's story, this story follows the linear structure.

**Rising Action**

The rising action is the place where everything begins building up to the turn of events. This is where the reader will understand the why and the what that was introduced in the exposition. The protagonist will be faced with conflict, which will lead them to the realization that their immediate goal will not be as simple to obtain as they originally thought; then, the character must begin to establish a New Goal. The rising action portion of the book should be tense and engaging, and the reader should begin to understand everything that is at stake for the protagonist. Character-driven scenes can be used to demonstrate what is at stake. An example of this would be a mother who is trying to shield her daughter from finding out she has magical powers in order to protect her from being discovered by forces of evil who will use her powers for themselves. Character-driven scenes lead to intense action scenes that keep the reader on the edge of their seat, rooting for the main character's success.

In the example of *The Three Little Pigs,* the Big Bad Wolf is introduced as a dangerous character who wants to eat the pigs. He watches them build from afar, plotting when he will attack. It is at this point in the story that the reader understands the why behind the pig. The pig who chose to take the time to construct a sturdy house of bricks. When the big bad wolf arrives, the pigs who built their houses of straw and sticks are faced with conflict (the Big Bad Wolf trying to break in and eat them, then blowing their houses down). This leads them to understand that their immediate goal, to build their houses quickly and return to business as usual, is not as practical as they thought. This part of the story contains the intensity necessary in the rising action part of the plot as the story approaches the climax.

**Climax**

The climax, or turning point, is the point in the story where the protagonist realizes what they must do in order to resolve the conflict. This is the part where the main questions the reader has developed throughout the course of the story are answered. At this point, all of the tension and emotion that has accumulated throughout the first part of the story will be released. This is when the story switches from building conflict to conflict resolution, and it is often the most engaging part of the story. It is important to keep readers on the edge of their seats by making them question whether or not the protagonist will come out on top and experience a happy ending. There should be some element of doubt present—a moment where all seems lost before the protagonist rises above the challenge and ends up on top. The climax is the point where the reader develops an even deeper admiration for the main characters as they observe the characters making brave decisions, learning an important lesson, persisting through challenge, and rising above.

Using our *Three Little Pigs* example, we see the emphasis switch from the main goals of the straw and stick pigs to the main goal of the brick pig. This is the part of the story where the brick pig becomes the hero by allowing the other two pigs into the sturdy brick house. Tension continues to mount as the wolf tries to blow the brick house down and fails, then begins plotting another way in. At this point, the brick pig exhibits vigilance and quick-wittedness while preparing for the Big Bad Wolf's next move. When the Big Bad Wolf attempts to come down the chimney of the brick house, readers are left on the edge of their seats, wondering if he will get in and eat the pigs after all. However, in the end, the brick pig is too smart, and the Big Bad Wolf is encountered by a pot of boiling water in the fireplace. The Three Little Pigs are safe at last—a happy ending in which the characters learn an important lesson about being patient, thorough, and smart.

## Falling Action

Everything that occurs after the climax is part of the falling action. The falling action should be in alignment with everything that has happened, leading up to that point, and it should feel inevitable. It must be directly tied to decisions and actions made previously, and the outcome should seem logical. This is the point where all the primary questions have been answered, and all conflicts have been resolved.

There are several versions of *The Three Little Pigs,* but one example of a falling action that can be seen in some of them is when the pigs engage in singing and dancing after the Big Bad Wolf has been defeated for good. As they dance around, carefree and enjoying themselves, the reader can see how the pig who made a house of bricks was right — patience is key. At this point in the story, all of the pigs are happy, safe, and unified together, and they are all benefiting as a result of the third pig's decision to build a sturdy house of bricks for protection, then place water on the fireplace to outsmart the Big Bad Wolf.

**Resolution/Denouement**

The final aspect of plot development is resolution or denouement. This draws all events, conflicts, and questions to a conclusion. This is the place where all of the loose ends are tied up by the lovers finally ending up together, the hero receiving recognition, or the adventurer returning home. This part of the book symbolizes a new, and generally improved, reality for all of the characters. At this point, the characters will have undergone great development as well and will have grown into wiser and improved versions of themselves who have successfully resolved the conflict they faced. This part of the story should be logical (do not introduce outlandish scenarios or new characters here) and leave the reader feeling satisfied.

The recognition the third pig receives in The Three Little pigs when the other two pigs express their gratitude for being protected and apologize for judging the third pig for working at a slower pace, is an example of resolution. At this part of the story, the reader can truly see how it all paid off and how the other two pigs have grown wiser and learned from their mistakes. Ultimately, the reader should arrive at this resolution feeling satisfied that all the pigs are safe, happy, and have learned a new life lesson.

**The Use of Subplots**

Although subplots are not the main idea of the story, developing subplots can be useful for supporting the main plot and highlighting the most crucial issues and themes at the heart of the story. An example of a subplot could be the protagonist's relationship with the shop owner down the street who always shows grace and kindness and holds space for people to share about their life issues. The development of this relationship over time could serve to drive in the story's key points about human relationships and a general understanding of the kinds of people the characters are.

### Clarifying Questions: Did Your Plot do its Job?

As you approach the end of your story writing process, it is important to go back and ask yourself several important questions to ensure that you have stayed on track with what you wanted to express in the plot. Have the characters changed over the course of the story in the way you hoped they would? What were the key areas of growth or learning for the characters? What led them to change? Did they achieve their goals? Lastly, did you stick to the core themes of the story (for example, true love always prevails)?

Going back once more to *The Three Little Pigs* example, the goal of the story is that taking your time to think things through will benefit you later. We can see that this has been clearly demonstrated over the course of the story in the way the two pigs who did not take their time learning from the third pig, who did. This is an area of character growth and learning for the pigs. It is also an area of triumph for the pig who was not afraid to go against the grain. At the end of the day, the third pig's goal, to live in a house sturdy and safe from dangers like the Big Bad Wolf, has been achieved. The theme of the story has been achieved by demonstrating how patience and thinking things through led to a happy ending for the pigs.

# Chapter 3: Step 3 - Defining the "Where" Through Setting

In order to draw your readers into the world you create in fiction; you must first have a profound understanding of what makes that world what it is. This is where developing a setting comes into place. When it comes to writing fiction, there is often much emphasis placed upon who the characters are, what they are doing, and what is happening to them and very little emphasis on the environment they are in. The setting is one of the most widely overlooked yet equally crucial components of fiction writing.

**Basics of Setting: What to Do and What Not to do**

Before setting out to develop your story setting, there are several things to keep in mind. First, when describing the setting, it is important to use all five senses. By describing exactly what the characters can see, hear, smell, taste, and feel, the reader will feel completely immersed in the story and where it goes next. The setting is not something that you can establish once and expect the reader to stay engaged throughout the rest of the book. It is important to spread setting descriptions out throughout the book in order to pull your reader into each moment truly. Whenever the plot is thickening or changing, and the character's actions need to be emphasized, that is a good time to provide new details of the setting.

While in-depth sensory descriptions of settings are crucial, there is a fine line between being thorough and over-describing. If you spend too long describing every tiny detail of the setting all at one time, your reader is sure to lose interest and become distracted. Not only this, but over-describing a setting may also stifle a reader's imagination, making it more difficult for them to envision the world in a way that is captivating to them.

**Location, Context, Social Era, Lifestyle**

Now that you are aware of how to approach the setting, let's talk about the details you'll need to provide in order to illustrate the bigger picture. First of all, you need to know the general location of your story. This involves the country, region, city/town, or planet (if your story takes place in another world). Once you have established a general location, you will break it down into smaller categories such as specific neighborhoods, households, or places of work or study. It is important to establish context around the social era the story is taking place in as well. If the story is happening during a post-war era, or in a city neighborhood that is being newly gentrified, those elements will greatly impact the journey. The journey of the characters and the unfolding of the plot. You must take into account any element of culture. What country, tribe, or community are your characters involved in? Do they have any special family traditions? What are the foods they eat? It is important to indicate the general social and political climates of the story, as well as how people interact with one another in different contexts.

## Geography and Population

Geography is an element of setting that goes hand-in-hand with a location as it pertains to the natural environment. Does your story take place in a mountain village, off the coast of Mozambique, in a corner of East Harlem, or in a galaxy far beyond our own? You must make your reader aware of both natural geography (oceans, rivers, forests, mountains) and man-made geography (bridges, monuments, buildings, cemeteries). Also, to be taken into account with geography is the population of a given setting. The character's experiences are likely very dependent on how many people live in their area. The experience of a character living in a small town, versus a city with several million people, versus an isolated island, will all be vastly different.

## Climate, Mood, Atmosphere

The climate of a setting goes along the same lines as its geography as well. It is important to establish the relationship between climate and people's moods and well-being. It is more common, for example, to see a relaxed and carefree lifestyle in a village community on the coast than in Seattle on the 200th cloudy day, or in the deep woods while a family struggles to survive during a harsh winter. The mood and atmosphere of a story are developed as the characters react to elements of their environment, including temperature, lighting, and other factors that can be detected by the five senses. Before each scene, be sure to take time to ask yourself what kind of mood you are striving to establish. What is the weather like? Is it sunny and serene, with puffy clouds in the sky? Or is it a gloomy day with whistling wind that makes the hairs on your arms stand up? If the story is occurring inside, what is the atmosphere of the room? Is it comfortable and cozy, or is there something unsettling about it?

**Time of Year, Time of Day, Passage of Time**

Time of year is another important element of setting, which includes seasons as well as important days. These days can be holidays, first days of work or school, or significant dates to the characters such as anniversaries, birthdays, dates of death, and dates of past historical events. Time of day is important for describing if events are happening at dawn, dusk, in the heat of the afternoon, or in the middle of the night. While it is not possible to take the reader on a moment-by-moment journey as it would be in real-time, it is absolutely crucial to account for elapsed time throughout the story. Flashbacks, foreshadowing, and in-between moments can all be used to allude to the passage of time and keep readers from becoming confused or feeling removed from the story.

## Establishing Setting in Fictitious Worlds

In the cases of fantasy and fictitious worlds, you will have a bit more work to do in order to draw your reader in and make them feel connected with the setting (as it is a world they have never seen). Begin by creating the world your story is occurring on. Does it resemble earth in any way? What are the major differences? Establish the name of the world, as well as how its creatures live and function. What is the terrain like? One very helpful tip for establishing this fictitious world is to draw a map. After you have developed a map of this world, you can narrow things down and determine in which particular settings the plot will unfold.

## Why is Setting Important?

One common misconception about the setting is that it is only the backdrop of the story. This is incredibly false. The setting is crucial to the development of a story because it includes everything that has to do with how the characters navigate through space, time, and social environments. Think about the places in your own life where you spend the most time, for example. If you spend most of your time on a college campus, it is likely that you have a favorite meal in the cafeteria, a favorite faculty or staff person who you look forward to talking to a favorite tree or bathroom stall, and a favorite place to study. It is also likely that there is a building or room that you rarely enter because it is rumored to be haunted, or because the meanest or creepiest staff or faculty person works there. This is just one example of how setting impacts the way we orient in the world and why it is so crucial to creating a good piece of fiction writing. Every component of the story setting is essential to building the mood and plot of the story. As well as how the characters grow and change within each context. Your setting should be clearly described using literary devices and descriptive language that can clearly draw a picture in your reader's mind to help them envision the environment.

When story setting is done right, it will help the plot to flow from one event to the next clearly and realistically. The story setting should align with the plot of the story. For example, if you are writing about a young musician who is struggling to get by and make it big in New York, you will want to describe the setting of his closet-sized apartment. Also, the streets where he feels unseen and the subways he falls asleep on every day as he travels home from the barista job that barely pays the bills. A rustic, mountain setting would not make sense for this plot.

**Further Benefits of Setting**

The setting also creates a sense of unity between the characters and the plot by describing why the characters do what they do and which elements of their environment lead them to be in certain situations. Additionally, setting draws the reader in to feel like they are truly in that place with the character, experiencing the same narrative and emotions.

The setting should be aligned with the main characters throughout the story. Going back to the example of the young musician. If his conflict is being withdrawn and not having the confidence to pursue his dream, it is likely he keeps his eyes down on the city streets and attempts to sit alone and mind his own business on the subway. However, if he is outgoing and willing to talk to anyone or do anything to fulfill his dream, even when that means failure, it is likely he is trying to talk to everyone and drop his name in any context he can. He may be trying to instigate conversations about his music with everyone he comes across and is likely to seize any opportunity to perform (at parks, in cafes, in bars, etc.). In this case, the character's conflict would not be a lack of confidence, but rather, lack of opportunity or being noticed.

### Establishing Setting Credibility

Just as it is important to establish credibility with character development, it is important to develop that same credibility with the development of particular settings. If you are trying to describe a real place that you have never been, it is crucial to do research on that place to make sure what you are describing is geographically and culturally accurate. If it is a place you can visit in person, that is the best way to get a real-life understanding of the setting. However, this is not always logistically possible. In those cases, you can make use of media resources such as Google Earth, YouTube, newspaper clippings, images/photographs, and encyclopedias. You may also do the same thing you did in the stages of character development, where you visit particular settings and take field notes on what you observe.

# Chapter 4: Step 4 - Selecting a Point of View

The point of view of fiction writing is the type of narration you choose to tell the story. When it comes to selecting a point of view for your fiction story, you have several options to choose from.

**First-Person Point of View**

The first-person point of view adopts the perception of a character, generally the main character, of a fiction story. This point of view records everything as it is witnessed and understood by the character, and uses pronouns such as I, me, and mine. This point of view is useful for giving the reader a closer look inside the mind of the character, letting the reader know exactly how they think and feel and allowing for a more personal connection between the reader and the character. This close connection is a major benefit to using the first-person point of view. One disadvantage is that you may not be giving your reader a well-rounded view of the setting and the other character's perceptions of things. This point of view is more personal but also more limited.

**Second-Person Point of View**

In the second-person point of view, the narrator speaks directly to the reader and adopts pronouns such as you, your, and yours to tell you your own story. In fiction writing, second-person is most commonly used to guide the reader through interactive books.

## Third-Person Objective Point of View

Third-person objective point of view is when a character serves as the narrator of the story but without any insight into their personal thoughts, feelings, and perception of what is going on. This point of view aims for neutrality through the use of third-person pronouns, and it is designed to be unbiased and give the reader the freedom to interpret what they are reading freely without the emotional response of the narrator.

## Third-Person Limited Point of View

Third-person limited point of view uses both third-person pronouns and insight into a particular character's emotions and perception of the world. In this point of view, all characters will be referred to in third-person, but only one (usually the main character) will be followed throughout the story from start to finish.

## Third-Person Omniscient Point of View

Third-person omniscient point of view is focused on giving the reader a point of view similar to that of a godly figure, looking down on everyone else and seeing what is happening. This point of view provides deep insight into the personal lives of several characters throughout the book, not just one character. In order to write in this point of view, you must be prepared to provide details of the emotional states, inner dialogues, perceptions, and actions of multiple characters.

### Dialogue vs. Narration

When thinking of how to write a point of view, you must understand how to use the tools. The tools of both dialogue and narration. Even if the narrative is being written in third-person, first-person pronouns are still used when dialogue is occurring between characters. This is why it is crucial to symbolize every phrase of dialogue with quotation marks to set it apart from the rest of the text.

### Point of View Toolbox: Moods and Dimensions

There are several tools available to you when deciding which point of view to use in a piece of fiction writing. Begin by asking yourself what type of story you are writing, and which sort of mood you hope to create. If you are writing a story designed to be suspenseful, you will be better off writing from a first-person perspective, as it is more limited and will inevitably create more tension. However, if you are writing a fantastical story about another dimension, you may choose to write from several third-person perspectives in order to give the reader a better understanding of the world.

**Using Your Own Voice**

The point of view you choose is also largely dependent on the journey of finding your own distinct style and voice to use in your writing. In order to develop your own strong writing voice, be sure to pay close attention to the differences in voices and points of view in the fiction stories you read. Ask yourself how you perceive different points of view differently. Which one sticks with you the most as a reader? While it is helpful to use the voices of other writers as inspiration, it is important not to attempt to imitate any other author's voice or force yourself to use any particular point of view. Trust your instincts. You know your story better than anyone!

**Clarifying Questions: Observation vs. Participation**

Several important questions to ask yourself before beginning are as follows. First of all, do you want your narrator to be involved in the events they tell about? Perhaps they are simply an observer of those events or are serving to reconstruct distant events with their narration. Is the narrator far removed from the story, or is there a lot at stake for them personally in the way things unfold? Lastly, is the narrator credible in telling the story? Can your reader trust that they have enough information and experience to portray the story accurately?

# Chapter 5: Step 5 - Defining the "Big Idea" Through Theme

When it comes to fiction writing, every story must have a deeper meaning. When the reader reaches the end of the story, what is the message or topical knowledge they will be taking away? If your story lacks a theme, it inevitably will be lacking the ability to establish meaningful connections between the characters and the plot, and the story itself will lack significance or memorability. The theme is a central element of fiction writing; it answers the question, "What is this story *really* about?". Before you proceed with a piece of fiction writing, you should be able to summarize the main purpose of your story in one sentence. One important distinguishing factor is that theme is not the same thing as the moral of the story. The moral of the story is a lesson the author wants the reader to take away, while the theme relates more heavily to the deeper significance of the story.

**Major Themes in Fiction Writing**

The most powerful themes are generally those which appeal to common interest or understanding. The theme "good trumps evil" is one of the most common themes in literature, which expresses that even when the battle is challenging, forces of good always come out on top at the end of the day. The theme of power struggles and dynamics are also popular, and such themes typically demonstrate that one must have secret powers or approaches in order to achieve dominance. A common theme is one that claims the freedom of humans and the challenges of living in a society that tries to limit that freedom. Contrarily, there is a common theme that expresses society as the saving grace. That protects humans from their natural, animalistic wickedness.

## Determining Your Theme(s)

Choosing a theme depends heavily on the general audience you are writing to, as well as the genre you are writing in. For example, the writings of romantic novelists would revolve around themes of love. Begin by determining the broad themes you plan to discuss (love, loss, power, loneliness, family, coming-of-age, self-discovery, mystery, the pursuit of happiness, etc.). You may determine that you want to write a cross-over of several themes, for example, the relationship between the pursuit of happiness, loss, and self-discovery. One way to maintain relevance to the theme is to base it heavily on your characters, setting, or plot. For example, if your protagonist is a professional female swimmer training to qualify for the Olympic team, your themes could have to do with competition, drive, the sport of swimming as a whole, the challenges that face women in athletics, or any combination of those. Ultimately, the theme is a summary of all the primary ideas of a story. Many great stories explore a variety of topics and subtopics, but it is important not to go so broad that your reader gets lost. A good rule of thumb is to select anywhere between two and five primary themes that your story will focus on. This will help you avoid getting off track and will keep your reader engaged. Lastly, although themes will vary between genres and intended audiences, it is important to select themes that are relatively universal and can appeal to people of all races, genders, cultures, lifestyles, ages, etc.


## Thematic Statements

Thematic statements based upon opinions or moral discoveries the characters express throughout a piece of fiction writing which communicate a deeper message to the reader. The thematic statement is what combines and summarizes the main topics of the book in a brief phrase. For example, if the themes of a book are love and equality, the thematic statement could be "love your neighbor as yourself." Thematic statements demonstrate how the theme plays out in the world. After you know what your thematic statements are, you can stay on track with the larger purpose of your story and eliminate the details which don't support that larger purpose. It is important to keep character arc in mind when developing thematic statements in order to draw the reader in with a sense of humanity. Thematic statements can be present in everything from the character's backgrounds to their current internal conflicts. When writing about your character's experiences, it is vital to ask yourself, "How is this experience going to impact the reader? What message is the reader going to take away from this?"

### The Use of Motif

A motif is a symbol, structure, or literary device that is recurring throughout a piece of fiction writing. Geography is one primary example of a motif. The themes in a story about a girl living on a Polynesian island and a teenage boy growing up in Baltimore, for example, would be very different. The elements of geography can play strongly into the reiteration of the theme throughout a story. Another common motif is the weather, and how changing weather patterns can represent a change in mood and expression of the theme.

### The Use of Symbol

A symbol is a particular object, image, figure, or character that represents a deeper meaning. An example of a symbol is the bow and arrow Katniss uses in *The Hunger Games*. While on the outside, this is an object used in battle, it is also a symbol that represents the depth of Katniss' stealth, skill, precision, and courage.

### The Relationship Between Theme and Character Development

As previously mentioned, a large part of theme development is dependent upon the character arc. It is vital to consider how the character's experiences, opinions, and morals relate to the overarching theme of the story. When considering the timeline of scenes and character interactions, it is important to ask yourself how they all contribute to the overarching theme. If your theme is "the concept of marriage," for example, and is focused on a young woman learning the lessons about marriage that the other women in her family never learned. It makes a lot of sense to provide a scene exploring her relationship with a single mother character who left her husband after he was unfaithful.

## Staying on Track

One of the biggest benefits of summarizing your primary themes from the beginning is that you can refer to it as a guide throughout the rest of the process (and subsequent development of motifs, symbols, and characterization). There is nothing worse than a piece of fiction writing that jumps from one scene to another in a chaotic manner that leaves the reader with questions and leaves them unable to identify the point of the story. Establishing your main themes ahead of time can help you avoid adding secondary characters, subplots, and random details that do not relate to what you are trying to convey. This skill, also called "cutting the fat," is necessary for keeping your reader from becoming lost, frustrated, or bored. Another useful tip for staying on track is to incorporate the primary theme(s) into your outline process, so you can have extra assuredness that each scene you write is relevant.

Because the theme is so dependent on other elements of fiction, such as the characters, plot, and setting, it is rare that writers are able to understand their theme from the beginning fully. Although you do want to establish primary themes to serve as a general guideline throughout the writing process, you may find that your theme will shift slightly as you go. If this happens, you must be prepared to re-evaluate and make adjustments accordingly to ensure that everything still flows.

**Out of the Box Tip for Theme Writing**

As previously mentioned, it's good to be able to summarize what your story is going to be about, and what some of the primary topics are, before you begin writing. That being said, many writers may find it inhibiting on their writing process to try to determine the theme before the story has even begun to take its course. In some instances, you may find it helpful to give yourself a brainstorming session in which you write down all of the possible topics and theme possibilities that lie within your story idea. You can loosely tie the primary topics into your planning process to keep you on track, but allow yourself some flexibility to let the main theme(s) of the story appear as you go. Although you will begin with some general ideas of what you want to express and what you want the reader to take away, it is a great idea to let the process guide you into creating a more concrete definition of your theme. Allow yourself to move with the flow of the story and watch how your theme(s) appear to you.

# Chapter 6: Step 6 - Developing Style and Finding Your Voice

The writing world is brimming with possibilities for self-expression and stylistic variation. The voice and style you develop in your fiction writing allows you to create worlds all your own, which can serve as reflections of your inner world and personal aspirations. When it comes to developing your personal voice and style in fiction writing, there are several important things to consider. This chapter will explore the most crucial elements on the journey of finding your personal style and voice.

## "Show, Don't Tell" with Style and Voice

As previously mentioned, it is important to leave room for the reader's imaginations by describing scenes with enough detail to both draw the reader in and inspire them to draw their own mental pictures. However, when it comes to developing style and voice, the way you choose to "show" is crucial. You should try to think outside the box when generating descriptions that stray from the typical perspectives. Ask yourself, "how can I apply my own personal twist to this perspective?" Another tip is to utilize expressive vocabulary. When using common adjectives, such as "beautiful" or "exciting," try searching for synonyms that can express the same thing in a more colorful way.

## Determine What Makes You Unique

Every person sees the world in a different way. Perspectives are formed through life experiences, and because every person has a different story, every person has a unique perspective. No matter how insignificant you may feel your perspective is, it is guaranteed that there are elements of your perspective that can provide a new way of understanding the world to your readers. A good starting question when it comes to defining your personal voice and style is: "what makes me unique?" You may find it helpful to create a list of things that contribute to your perspective and who you truly are, from which to draw your personal style in writing. If you are a typically "romantic" person, allow that perspective to infiltrate your writing and create romantic storylines with your own unique twist. While your unique qualities may be as broad as a particular personality type or passion, they may also be narrow, such as your quirks, habits, guilty pleasures, strange fears, special objects, obsessions, or what brings you comfort. Allow the unique qualities you notice in yourself and other people to play a role in the way you detail the characters in your story. Perhaps you are writing about a character who wears glitter on their eyelids every day, has a nervous habit of shaking their pen when they or thinking, or who has a trademark way of greeting people. As mentioned in the Character chapter of this guide, such qualities are endearing and help the reader to build a personal connection with the characters in fiction writing.

## Be Authentic

When you allow yourself to be completely authentic in your writing, you will quickly distinguish yourself as a writer. Some writers are known for writing with an element of suspense. At the same time, others write from a mystical perspective or explore the depths of the feminine. The sign of pure and engaging authenticity is to draw readers in so far that they forget what they are reading is fabricated. Over time, this engagement will lead to increased fiction writers developing their own unique presence in the writing world and becoming known for what they bring.

## Be Original

Another crucial element to establishing your style and voice is to avoid clichés. If you are trying to imitate another storyline or style of writing, your writing will be dry and unoriginal, and it will ultimately lose the reader's interest. It is important to trust your own experiences and perspective enough to let it guide your writing process and avoid clichés. If you find yourself writing a phrase or following a storyline that seems like something you have heard before, it is a good idea to choose another direction to travel in.

## Activating the Senses

One of the key elements of discovering your voice and personal style is to integrate sensory experiences into your writing. In order to draw your readers into the story, you must write in a way that illicit emotion and floods your reader with imagery to keep them engaged. To appeal to your reader's senses, you must write in a way that appeals to your own. When illustrating a scene, ask yourself what the character sees, what they hear, what they smell, and what they feel. As human beings, we are all attuned to different details of daily life. This personal attunement gives writers the ability to describe two very similar experiences in a completely different way, thus immersing the reader in a sensory experience unique to that author's perception of things. Allow your personal attunement to certain things to fuel your writing process and set you apart.

## Spicing Things Up with Metaphor

A great way to unleash your creative side in fiction writing is to create metaphors out of everyday objects. This exercise can be applied to any object in your line of vision. Ask yourself about the backstory of that particular object, giving it a past, present, and future. Ask yourself, "What could this object stand for beyond its general purpose?" Consider, for example, a chipped coffee mug on the shelf of a thrift store. Day after day, people come in shopping for mugs, but every time they pick up this particular one, they end up putting it back because it's chipped. When someone eventually decides to purchase the mug in spite of the chip, this could serve as a representation of giving new chances and finding the value in brokenness.

## The Importance of Intimacy

The more you invite the reader into a written experience, the more of an impact your writing will have on that reader. Your descriptions of setting and character should include minute details, which can help place the reader even deeper in the story and help them to feel like they are part of it. Seemingly insignificant details, such as the sound of the wind rustling and the branches of a tree brushing against the upstairs window, help the reader to put themselves in the character's shoes and experience the emotions the character experiences. Intimate details are another tool for distinguishing your writing style and truly bringing the reader into your world.

## How Personal Experience Influences Voice

A common misconception among writers is that in order to generate fiction, you have to stay far away from any experiences that resemble your own. In reality, quite the contrary is true when it comes to fiction writing. Personal experience can serve as an excellent starting line for the journey of a fiction story. From here, you can draw inspiration from real people, emotions, life memories, and personal philosophies. Writing from this place creates space for empathy and authenticity in the story, which is sure to draw readers in and allow them to build an emotional connection with what they read.

Not only can you base some characters, elements of plot, setting, or theme, off of things you have experienced in your life, fiction also gives you the freedom to change details or elaborate in any way you choose! In fiction writing, you have the opportunity to use your personal life as a basic guideline, then let your imagination get to work in carrying the rest of the story. There is plenty of room for imagination and theoretical situations in relation to personal experiences, and the best fiction writers take advantage of this and allow it to influence their personal style and voice. Because every person's life is unique, so then can the way those experiences impact their writing.

## Practice Writing Every Day

Coming to terms with personal experiences, memories, dreams, and philosophies is not a simple process. Humans beings are incredibly complex and constantly changing based upon what happens in their lives. One of the best ways to sift through experiences and find what you strive to express in your writing is by participating in writing every single day. When you sit down to write, try to do so without any expectations or plans in mind. Allow yourself to free-write without paying attention to any of the typical rules of writing. Allow your soul to pour out on the page, then allow yourself to be inspired by what comes from it. Over time, you will begin to notice recurring themes, philosophies, and passions, making an appearance in what you write about. Your free writings can serve as inspiration for the situations your fiction characters experience and the lessons they learn.

# Chapter 7: Step 7 - Uncovering the Secrets of Good Fiction Writing

Now that you have covered each of the elements of fiction writing. You are almost ready to be on your way. However, any writer can follow the tips and information provided in definitions of each element of fiction. It is not by simply following the previous steps that you will become a strong and memorable fiction writer. In order to become truly distinguished, there are a few secret techniques to bear in mind.

1. Read, read, read. The more you indulge in personal reading endeavors, the more you will be able to identify the elements of fiction in practice. You will become familiar with the literary devices, style, and voice used by various authors. Pay attention to how certain stories make you feel and what you take away, and approach each of your own projects with the energy you hope to make your reader experience and what you want them to learn.

2. Dare to ask yourself, "What if?" and "What next?" Dare to dream about what you can create in your fictional world. If 'X' happens, what will happen to 'Y'? Give yourself space to think of all possible outcomes.

3.  Take risks and immerse yourself in new environments. If you stay in the same place, doing the same thing, the writing you can base upon your personal experiences may begin to dwindle. Challenge yourself to try new things and visit new environments, and take notes each time you do. How might the observations of this new environment create a unique story idea?

4.  Give yourself time to soak in the process. As writers, it is easy to feel a rush to get new stories generated as quickly as possible. This can be a critical mistake. In order to create a story that will stick with the reader, bring joy to your soul, and enrich your experience as a writer and a human being, you need to have the patience to let yourself ruminate in the writing process. This can come by way of sitting in quiet and pondering past memories and experiences of your life, which are fueling your stories, daydreaming about mystical worlds from which your story settings are drawn, or simply sitting at the moment and letting images and ideas flow freely onto the paper. Not only will giving yourself time and being present make your personal experience more enjoyable and lifechanging, but it will also refine your story and make it a true masterpiece.

5.  Aim to write what has never been written before. Every writer has the capacity within themselves to create something

completely unique using their personal style and voice, but this takes courage. You must be vulnerable with the parts of yourself that long to come to the surface. Allow yourself to engage with them and let them flow forth in your works. Learn from your own process, be inspired by what comes. This is the only way to inspire others with your writing truly.

6. When you are describing scenes in fiction writing, pay attention not only to the descriptive words you use but how they flow together. Language has the ability to create rhythm with the way it flows together. Read your descriptive sentences aloud, changing words as needed until the rhythm and sounds reflect the mood.

7. Maintain an obligation to yourself. Although the goal of a writer is always to keep readers engaged, the primary goal at the end of the day should be to yourself. How can you write the stories that are on your soul? How can you say the things that you have been given the words, experience, and passion to say? At the end of the day, what your writing does for you personally is the most important thing.

8. Life is about choices, and life stories are no exception. Before setting out to write any story, consider the series of choices the characters will make. Why do the characters make certain

choices, and what impact do those choices have on how the story unfolds?

9.  Determine particular "writing spaces" for yourself. Each time you set out to write, ask yourself where you need to be. You may take inspiration from writing in a garden, on a rooftop, in a junkyard, next to a country road, hunkered at a corner table of your favorite coffee shop, or settled at a writing desk you have created for yourself with things that inspire you. No matter where it is, make sure that you are in a space where your surroundings can inspire you and put your mind and spirit in the place they need to be.

10. Just get started. You may find yourself writing ten, fifty, or several hundred pages that don't end up going anywhere. That is part of the process. The hardest part of creating a fiction story is often simply choosing to get started. Decide to do that, and give yourself grace and patience as you observe where the process goes from there. Mistakes are a crucial part of the process, and you often have to sift through a lot of ideas and type many words before realizing where you are really trying to go.

# Conclusion

Throughout this guide, you were provided with the ins and outs of fiction elements, including the basic elements, things to avoid, and tips to apply to your writing process. At this point, you not only have an interest in writing fiction that inspired you to start these 7 steps, but also the tools to embark on the journey that is fiction writing.

At the beginning of this guide, you learned how to develop characters with whom readers can relate and establish emotional connections. You learned how to add depths to characters and to make their personal growth journey engaging for the reader. Next, you learned about the elements of the plot, and how to prepare your story by establishing a character's main and new goals, conflict, and eventual resolution that leaves the reader feeling satisfied. You learned that setting is not just something that sits in the background of the story, but rather an incredibly dynamic force in the way the story plays out. You learned how to discern between the various points of view and how to select one based on your purposes. You then explored the possibilities of theme, and how to stay on track with what your story is truly about. After this, you examined how to cultivate your personal writing style and voice, largely depending on your past experiences and personal values. Lastly, you were provided with ten out-of-the-box secrets for improving your fiction writing.

This guide is not the endpoint of your journey to fiction writing— it is just the beginning. Now that you have familiarized yourself with the elements and secrets of fiction writing, you can continue to use this guide as a map; you refer back to throughout your process. Now is your time to change the world through the worlds you create in fiction writing.

# Book 3: How to Write Non-Fiction

*7 Easy Steps to Master Creative Non-Fiction, Memoir Writing, Travel Writing & Essay Writing*

Jaiden Pemton

# Introduction

Welcome to "How to Write Non-Fiction". In this guide, we are going to explore how to create an exciting and engaging narrative that will captivate your readers. In particular, we are going to discuss how you can write effectively so that your readers can find your content easily digestible.

You see, the difference between good writing, and great writing, is in the way you get your message across. Many times, getting your message across is about putting yourself in your reader's shoes. When you do this, you're able to transport your readers straight into your state of mind. This is what creates an authentic reading experience.

Now, most people believe that writing non-fiction is about using academic-style prose. As such, the aim is to sound smart. This is why many non-fiction writers try their hardest to sound as smart as they can. However, this is a misconception. You don't need to sound "smart" to be a successful non-fiction writer. All you need to do is transmit the enthusiasm you have for your chosen topic. Then, you can create compelling writing that will leave readers wanting more.

In each of the chapters in this guide, we'll look at a major step in the creative writing process. It's important to note that each step builds on the previous one. In the end, you will have a winning formula once you put them all together. You will learn a successful system that has been proven to work time and time again.

So, what are you waiting for?

Let's get started with this journey into a world filled with exciting moments. After all, writing should be an enjoyable process. It should be the type of endeavor that will leave you feeling happy and satisfied with the type of content you are able to produce. Plus, you surely have something to share with the world.

That's what makes writing such a rewarding experience.

Please don't look at writing as a job. If you do so, it will become a chore, a burden if you will. As such, please take the time to go through each of the steps in this guide. You will find that writing will become one of the most rewarding and satisfying experiences you can even engage in.

Please bear in mind that the most successful writers are the ones who can convey their passion for a given topic. This passion is transmitted through their keen sense of communicating their thoughts and ideas. The best part is that this is a skill that can be developed. Therefore, anyone can develop the skills needed to be a successful writer.

Happy writing!

# Chapter 1: Step 1 - Deciding on Your Narrative

All great books tell a story. Now, you might think that type of approach is reserved for fiction writing. After all, fiction is, by definition, telling a story. While this is completely true, you will find that telling a story is not just reserved for fiction. Non-fiction works can also tell a story. In fact, non-fiction writing should tell a story. The reason for this is the need for creating a narrative.

When you write in the non-fiction domain, you must strive to create a consistent narrative that can deliver meaning and value to readers in an enjoyable format. This implies that you must avoid sterile discussions. Such discussions leave readers lacking a personal touch throughout the content. Therefore, it is essential for you to find a consistent narrative that reflects your true self.

In this chapter, we are going to look at the elements you need to create a consistent narrative that will enable you to engage readers in such a way that your content resonates with them. Best of all, you will find that you don't need exceptional skills to make this type of approach perfectly plausible.

### Finding Your True Voice

Often, you hear writing coaches tell their students they need to find their true voice. However, that is vague, especially if you don't know how to bring your inner voice out. Finding your inner voice is about channeling your personality. When writing, you don't need to pretend to be someone you're not.

This is one of the biggest mistakes that novice writers make.

You see, novice writers attempt to sound smart and sophisticated. This approach leads them to labor through writing tasks as they search for complex vocabulary and grammatical structures. The truth is that readers don't expect to find uber-complex language when they pick up a book. In fact, many readers simply want an enjoyable read that will leave them with the information they seek.

Here is a great exercise you can do to help you find your voice.

When you set out to write on any given topic, sit down, and write. Just write. Don't think about what others will think. Just write down your ideas. You can write as much or as little as you like. A good starting point on one page.

Once you've written your first page, stop and read it. When you read it, you will get a glimpse of the way you sound, that is, your inner voice. Of course, you would have to clean it up. After all, it is extremely rare for a writer to produce flawless content on the first try. The aim here is to simply become comfortable with your own voice.

Then, take the time to write more and more. As you write, pay attention to the type of words you use. Also, check out the type of sentences you build. You will immediately find a consistent pattern. This is your voice. As you uncover your voice, you will need to take care of appropriate grammar, spelling, and vocabulary. This is especially important if you're writing on a technical topic.

These first few pages may never see the light of day. They may remain filed away in your computer forever. However, they are the beginning of your journey as a writer. They will serve to help you find your voice. The most important thing to keep in mind is that you're not writing to please others. You're writing to get a message across.

**All About Grammar, Spelling, and Vocabulary**

Letting your hair down is a major step toward becoming a successful writer. However, you must ensure that you follow the proper grammatical guidelines of the English language. Of course, there is a place for certain devices such as the use of slang or informal expressions. Nevertheless, you must ensure that you use the proper vocabulary and expressions you need based on your chosen topic.

When it comes to grammar, it is important to make sure that you're using the right verb tense and sentence structure. Please keep this in mind as grammatical mistakes are the first thing that people will call you out on. Such mistakes might turn off some readers. Others may dismiss your writing entirely. While it is possible to have a mistake at some point, too many mistakes will definitely get you in trouble.

So, it's a good idea to enlist the help of an editor. You can get a trusted friend or family member to go over your writing. If you would rather get an objective third-party, you can hire a freelance editor to give your writing a look. You can find them on sites such as Fiverr. Also, you can use editing software to double-check your work. In the end, the software can help you pinpoint mistakes that you may not have caught.

As for spelling, word processing software generally checks this for you on the fly. As such, you can rely on your word processor of choice to give you a hand. In case you in doubt, a good old-fashioned dictionary will come in handy. Often, there are words and terms that even sophisticated software does recognize. So, it makes sense to have a handy reference guide. That way, you can be sure that you're getting the right spelling. If you happen to use words from other languages such as Latin or Greek, always take the time to double-check the terms. That way, you can be sure you're right on the mark.

Regarding vocabulary, please ensure that you have the right terminology. This is particularly important if you're writing on a technical subject. Often, there are specific terms that you may not be sure about. Also, things might get confusing with definitions. As such, it's always good to review that you're using the right definitions and interpretations of words.

**Finding the Right Pace**

Non-fiction writing can be tricky in terms of pacing. It can be quite tough to find an appropriate pace. After all, you run the risk of moving along too fast or moving along too slowly. When you fail to find the appropriate pace, readers may feel they are not getting their money's worth.

Think about it along with these terms.

In non-fiction writing, it is essential that you get to the point. Sure, you can write short introductions to present the topic. However, the sooner you get to the point, the better. When you're exploring a specific topic, the last thing you want is to drag out explanations and descriptions. Often, it's best to limit the length of definitions and focus more on examples. Also, descriptions need to be as concise as possible.

The biggest temptation here is to provide lengthy and elaborate explanations. While providing details is certainly useful, there is a limit to the level of detail you need to provide. Granted, there are topics that require a high degree of detail. In such cases, your experience and intuition will tell you how detailed you need to be. After all, you're the expert on the topic. Nevertheless, it's always best to keep things as simple as possible.

It is also important to consider your audience. Depending on the people you're writing for, you might need to slow down or speed up. For example, if you're writing a guide for beginners, you might want to slow things down and provide a greater level of detail. If you're writing a guide for experienced users, then you can certainly move along quicker.

A good rule of thumb here is to check out other books and content similar to what you are looking to produce. By comparing these other materials, you can get an idea of what works and what doesn't. That can provide you a good yardstick by which to measure your own writing. In the end, there is nothing wrong with drawing comparisons when you're new to writing.

Over time, your experience and intuition will provide you with the proper feel for the pacing you need to keep throughout your book. Moreover, you'll know where to slow down, when to pick things up, and when to really drill down.

Please bear in mind that your inner voice should make itself manifest. This means that your voice will be the reflection of your knowledge and experience. Ultimately, you can provide readers with an adequate sense of your mastery of the topic. That will produce a sense of security among your readers. They will come to recognize you as an authority on the subject.

**Maintaining a Consistent Narrative**

Please keep in mind that building a consistent narrative is essential in successful writing. For example, if you have a clear position on an issue, make sure you maintain this position. Flip-flopping on issues will most likely confuse your readers.

When you write guides or how-to materials, it's always a good idea to maintain consistent use of tone, grammar, vocabulary, and pacing. For instance, using complex vocabulary with an academic tone at the beginning of the book and then shifting to an informal tone with the use of slang, later on, will serve to create an inconsistent dynamic in your book. Therefore, maintaining a consistent narrative through your materials will lead readers to feel comfortable with your writing. In the end, they will come to trust you as they get a clear glimpse into your psyche. Ultimately, this will create the right environment for the materials you want to present to your readers.

# Chapter 2: Step 2 – Defining Your Purpose

When setting out to write, you must find your purpose. There must be a clear purpose for your writing. Otherwise, your content might come off as a rant with no clear direction. Naturally, that's the last thing you want to get across. Therefore, your writing needs to convey a clear message. When you do that, your readers will derive value from your words. In the end, your writing becomes a valuable source of knowledge and information.

In this chapter, we are going to look at finding your purpose. This is one of the most crucial elements any time you set out to write. When you have a clear purpose, writing becomes that much easier. As such, your inner voice will manage to find its way through to your audience in a clear and easy-to-follow manner.

**How to Find Your Purpose**

The first question you need to ask yourself is "why?" Generally speaking, you need to ask yourself why you are setting out to write. The answer to this question will reveal the type of approach you need to take. For example, some professionals set out to write a book as a means of positioning themselves in their chosen profession. Others write because they feel it's a way of letting their feelings out. Others write because they feel passionate about an issue. Therefore, they feel that writing about that issue will raise awareness of it.

Regardless of your specific purpose, you must ask yourself why you want to write in the first place. From there, you can derive the approach you need to get your message across. Consequently, your message is the second step in this process. You must ask yourself what your message is. This concept boils down to figuring out what you want your readers to take away from your materials.

Once you have your purpose and message clearly defined, the last step is to determine your audience. This is essential as the tone of your writing needs to reflect your audience. Naturally, writing for a younger audience would require you to use a more youthful and informal tone. In contrast, writing for an older audience would require a more formal tone.

Ultimately, your approach will depend on all three factors outlined here. By taking the time to think about them thoroughly, you will make the actual writing process easier for you.

**Types of Purposes**

There are different types of purposes for writing. Understanding them will give you a good idea of what approach you can take. So, let's discuss them in greater detail.

### *Writing to Inform*

This is the type of writing you can use to present information on any given topic. When you write to inform, you are simply presenting facts and information. For example, you can write a how-to guide, describe historical events, or simply discuss an issue. Ultimately, you want to maintain a neutral position, especially if you want to spark debate among readers.

Writing to inform is also about making sure you get the fact straight. Therefore, accurate information is a must. This also means getting definitions and terms right. Moreover, you want to make sure that you know your audience. That way, you can tailor your style to suit the age and background of your readers.

### *Writing to Persuade*

There are times when you write to get a specific point across. In such cases, your point might be to persuade your readers on a position in a given issue. Thus, you need to present a convincing argument based on the facts you present. Generally speaking, writing to persuade requires an engaging tone that's meant to awaken your reader's interest. In this type of writing, using creative descriptions is always best. Having a deep level of detail is essential to defeating any qualms your readers might have. In the end, your argument is so convincing that readers will be swayed in your direction.

### *Writing to Raise Awareness*

When you write to raise awareness on an issue, you need to communicate a specific sense of urgency. There are cases in which you want to address an extremely urgent matter. Hence, you need to cut straight to the chase. Very little introduction or background is needed. What readers expect in such cases is a quick rundown of facts. These facts are intended to highlight your position. As such, there will be no denying the importance of the issue you discuss. Here, a quick, fast-paced approach is a must.

### *Writing to Advertise*

Some materials are intended to advertise a product or service. With these materials, it's important to underscore a problem and then show how the product or service provides a solution. Often, companies write books and papers on the most pressing issues for their customers. Then, products and services are presented as a solution to these issues. In the end, the company closes with a call to action. Readers are then compelled to learn more about the company's solutions to their problems. This type of writing needs to be persuasive and filled with actionable information readers can use to find a solution to their needs.

As you can see, the various types of writing can help you create valuable materials. Depending on your specific purpose, you might end up with a combination of all of these approaches. The main thing to keep in mind is your main purpose and the message you're looking to get across.

## Getting the Right Message Across

All too often, writers get sidetracked and lose sight of their message. As such, it is essential that you keep your eyes on the prize at all times. Once you define what your message is, you need to make sure that comes across.

Let's look at an example.

You're a professional that aims to write a white paper outlining your customers' biggest problems. Therefore, your purpose is to inform, but also to advertise. As such, you want to list your customers' problems in a clear and direct manner. Something like a "top 5" or the "Three Biggest Problems" works very well to pique readers' interest. As you go through each problem, the idea is to be neutral. You want to avoid creating a negative feeling in the mind of your customers. If you do, they won't look at your products as a solution. They will look at your products as a result of the problem.

Next, outline how your product can help your customers solve their problems. Now, you want to be careful not to make any outrageous claims. But you do want to present your argument in a way that all readers can see the benefits of your product. Here, you want to provide a solid level of detail. That way, the virtues of your product will become evident.

Lastly, close out with a call to action. Something like, "visit our website to learn more" is a great way of moving from an informative approach to a selling one. In the end, your readers will find value in the information you provide, while also leading them to purchase your products.

In this example, we have a combination of writing to inform and persuade. Naturally, you want your readers to purchase your product. However, keeping a neutral and informative tone is a great way of helping your future customers see the value of your products. Otherwise, you might turn some customers off if they see you're simply peddling something.

**Always Stay Positive**

Keeping a positive attitude is always critical. Even if you're dealing with serious issues like climate change, you still want to maintain a positive mindset. Sure, it's important to stress the importance of serious issues. Nevertheless, attempting to evoke fear or outrage in our audience will only take you so far.

Think about this situation.

A pest control company writes a brochure about their services. The company goes on about how termites can destroy a house. If customers don't act quickly, pests might bring their house crashing down.

On the surface, that looks like effective marketing. However, customers may seek this company out of fear. In the end, customers will associate the company with a negative feeling. To maintain a positive attitude, the company can list the dangers that termites pose to a house. As such, the company is the leading source for pest control services. Ultimately, this company has the solution to any type of problem.

Do you see the difference?

The aim is to inform you about a problem by listing the potential dangers. The idea is to provide accurate information and not create panic. Then, the company presents its services as the ultimate solution to the problem. As a result, the company is associated with a solution and not the result of a terrible situation.

Please keep in mind that maintaining a positive attitude at all times is the best way for you to ensure that you're writing is always associated with positive feelings. Unless you're writing a horror novel, you should always strive to have your readers associate your content with positive feelings. This will ensure that your readers get valuable information while you position yourself as a leading source in your chose field. That's the best approach you can use to keep your readers on your side.

# Chapter 3: Step 3 - Determining your Audience

A critical aspect of effective writing knowing who will read your materials. Successful writers are keen on adapting their writing style to suit whomever their intended audience is. This makes it easier for them to communicate with readers.

Knowing who your audience depends on a few key factors. That is why this chapter is all about determining what your audience is. Moreover, you will find that once you figure out who your audience is, you can tweak your style as needed.

So, let's jump right into it!

**It Starts with the Topic**

The starting point should always be your topic. The topic itself will tell you quite a bit about the audience you'll be catering to. This is important to note as not everyone is interested in the same topics. For example, if you're writing a knitting guide, chances are you're not going to attract many guys. By the same token, a car repair book would not attract too many ladies. Now, this isn't to say that these topics are gender exclusive. What we are saying is that certain topics cater to one specific group of people more than another.

Of course, there are cross-cutting topics that everyone would be interested in reading. For instance, books on saving money are always popular regardless of people's specific demographics. The point here is to ensure that that you have a good idea of who would be interested in reading your content.

Also, please keep in mind that some topics are considered "niche" topics. These topics cater to a very specific group of individuals. As such, these groups possess very clear characteristics that you need to consider. A good example of this is sports. While sports, as a whole, are generally quite popular, individual sports may become niche topics. After all, how many fans does curling have compared to soccer? These are considerations that you must take into account when determining your audience.

**Age and Gender**

One of the most important aspects to consider is age. Naturally, some topics are more attractive to younger people than to older folks, and vice-versa. You can figure out what topics folks are interested in by doing an online search. You can search for something like, "most popular books teens" to uncover what types of topics are trending among teenagers.

Also, going on online platforms such as Amazon can reveal what types of books are most popular. There, you can see the topics that most readers are into. That should give you an indication of the types of readers your content can resonate with.

As for gender, there are specific topics that resonate with males more than females and vice-versa. As such, some common sense can go a long way with this demographic. However, you might be surprised to find that some topics have cross-cutting appeal. These are topics that would interest people from all walks of life. Topics such as health and fitness, finance, and self-development all have cross-cutting appeal. Nevertheless, you will find more gender-specific topics even within the broader scope of such topics.

**Tone and Approach**

When putting pen to paper, your readers' level of education plays an important role in determining the type of prose you aim to utilize. In this regard, you need to determine if you're writing for a general audience or a more specific one. In the case of academic publications, you need to maintain a tone consistent with more complex and abstract language.

However, if you're writing for a general audience, you might want to keep a more standard tone. By the same token, general audiences appreciate a more neutral tone, that is, using gender-neutral pronouns while avoiding any direct references to specific characteristics otherwise required in the topic. For example, you can address your readers directly by saying "you," while avoiding gender-specific pronouns like "he" or "she." In such cases, you can opt for the use of "they."

A good rule of thumb to keep in mind is to sound as natural as possible. If you normally speak with a more laid-back tone, then that should be your default tone. Also, if you're more inclined to speak in a formal tone, then make sure you get that message across, too. The main idea here is to avoid trying to be someone you're not. Often, this is the biggest mistake that novice writers make in the early going. Your natural voice will surely resonate with your target audience quickly and easily.

### Leveraging Social Media

Social media is the place to be now if you want to know what's in, and what's out. Being relatively active on social media can give you the opportunity to see what's trending. Also, you can stay up to date with the latest news and information. As such, you can leverage social media to get a great idea of how your potential readers react to specific situations.

If you already have a following, then social media is the best way for you to stay in touch with them. As you interact with your followers, you can get specific insight into who they are and what they are interested in. This is crucial when it comes to tailoring your style to suit their needs.

Fiction writers love to interact with their readers. In doing so, they can gain an understanding about readers' interests, expectations, and demands. Believe it or not, your readers will demand certain things from you. In some cases, these demands surrounding events or characters. In others, your readers may ask you to write about specific topics. This is especially true in the non-fiction domain.

Another great way that writers leverage social media is to ask their readers to suggest topics they would like to read about. This is a great way of giving people what they want. Many times, readers have specific questions they would like you to answer for them. If you can provide those answers, your readers will surely follow you. So, do take the time to interact with your readers on social media whenever possible.

### Capitalizing on Trends

Every now and then, events occur that capture news headlines and most people's attention. These events permeate the social landscape for any given length of time. These are wonderful opportunities for you to write on issues most people are interested in.

When you look to capitalize on trends, you need to pick a position and run with it. For example, let's assume you're looking to write on a current political issue. You may choose to remain neutral and just inform on the matter. That's perfectly fine. However, you must ensure that you always remain neutral. On the other hand, you might choose to state your position and write from that perspective. Therefore, your writing would have to be geared toward those folks who subscribe to your specific position. That means using the type of language and tone that is consistent with those folks.

Also, you must consider the overall profile of your readers. For instance, if you're address trends more popular with younger audiences, then you need to keep and light, fast-paced approach. Please bear in mind that younger individuals may not have the luxury of sitting down to read a long article. By the same token, your work might be oriented toward older individuals. These folks may have more time to devote to reading. Therefore, you can afford to make your point more elaborately.

Please keep in mind that any time you address current events, you must try to stay on the cutting edge. Thus, it's crucial for you to ensure that you present information that's consistent with your readers' wishes and desires. Ultimately, the topic itself doesn't really matter. What does matter is the way that you present it to your audience?

**Important Considerations**

Whenever you set out to write, it's always a good idea to put yourself in your readers' position. After all, you need to produce content that people would actually like to read. Often, this means putting yourself on the other side of the ball. Always ask yourself, "why would anyone read this?" The answer to this question can serve as a means of producing relevant content.

It's important to learn from mistakes. If previous content wasn't successful, you need to figure out why it didn't take off. That analysis will enable you to make changes so that your readers can get what they expect. Ultimately, it's about meeting your readers' expectations consistently so that you can continue to gain momentum in your following.

Lastly, please keep in mind that your readers change over time. With changing trends and situations, you might find that a winning combination may need to be altered. Therefore, it's always a good idea to stay in touch with your audience. That way, you can find out what they need and how you can deliver it to them. This is why staying in touch with readers is always a great idea. Successful writers build email lists. Then, they encourage their readers to submit questions and any suggestions. In doing so, you can ensure a constant feedback loop that allows you to find a great way of discovering new topics to keep you relevant.

Please bear in mind that successful writers always deliver what their readers want. That's the bottom line. If you can do that, you will always have a winning combination regardless of the topic itself. In the end, you will engage your readers in such a way that your communication will only continue to get stronger.

# Chapter 4: Step 4 - Outlining Chapters Effectively

Proper organization is critical when it comes to writing a great book. Many times, novice writers commit a huge mistake by not properly organizing their content. Organizing content is all about ensuring that you have an adequate pace and flow to the way the material is presented. In other words, you have an appropriate setup, thereby ensuring your readers will have no trouble following your lead.

The entire organization process begins with outlining chapters based on the amount of information you wish to cover. Naturally, larger books with more content will need more chapters than books with less content. As a result, you need to be aware of how many sections you need to break your book down into.

In this chapter, we are going to take a look at how you can organize your content effectively while ensuring the overall flow of the material.

**Understanding the Scope of Your Project**

The single most important thing you need to consider when starting your project is its scope. By "scope," we mean the amount of material that you wish to cover. For example, if you're looking to cover a good chunk of material, then you are looking at a broader scope. If you're looking to cover less content, then you are looking at a narrower scope.

Please bear in mind that it's quite easy to get sucked into pushing for a broader scope. This can happen if you're not disciplined enough to write up an outline and then stick to it. This generally occurs when writers don't have a clear sense of where they are going. This is why you must ensure that you have a clear idea of where you want your project to go.

Consider this situation:

You are writing a book on holiday decorations. At first, you wish to focus solely on Christmas decorations. Then, you realize that Halloween decorations are also fun to do. So, you add those to the book. After that, you figure that Easter decorations would also be good. And so, you keep adding to the book.

Now, there is nothing wrong with the amount of information you plan to include in your book. The problem is that you never had a clearly defined scope. As such, your book appears to be a collection of random items all mashed together. Perhaps a better approach would have been to create separate volumes. For instance, one volume would focus solely on Christmas decorations, then the second on Halloween, the third on Easter, and so on.

In this example, you will find that simply adding and adding to your book will create a mix of ideas that may not necessarily fit well together once joined. So, do make sure that you have the right scope in mind when setting out to write your book.

## Outlining Chapters

Once you have determined your scope, that is how much you plan to cover, you can move on to breaking down your content into chapters. A chapter is essentially a very broad idea that you will develop. In this development, you can break down the idea into as much detail as possible given the constraints you have. These constraints are limited to time and space. As for time, you might be on a deadline. As such, writing too much can negatively affect the time you have to complete the project. The second constraint is space. For instance, you may be working with a specific number of words. Therefore, you can't afford to ramble on too much. Otherwise, you'll run out of words.

To outline your chapters, all you need to do is break down your topic into subtopics. Each subtopic represents the main idea about the topic. These main ideas are important pieces that must be put together in order to assemble the entire puzzle.

There are no specific rules or guidelines on how many chapters should be in a book or the specific word count. This decision is based on your expertise and experience as a writer. A good rule of thumb is to break your main topic into about three to five main ideas. From there, you can use them to plan each chapter.

Now that you have your chapters outlined, then you can go on to decide the actual content that will be included in the chapter. This is largely a tactical decision, meaning that you'll choose what to include and what not, once you're in the writing process. For instance, many writers choose to leave out specific content that isn't directly related to their overall idea. Others choose to add content that they have not thought of before.

Please bear in mind that this organization is not set in stone. However, you must try your best to stick to your original plan as much as possible. That way, you can reduce the amount of wasted time spent on a topic.

**How to Determine What Stays and What Goes**

As mentioned earlier, the actual words you write in each chapter are a game-time decision. Some writers like to be very detailed. As such, they outline everything that will be included in the chapter. Others are less proactive. So, they don't actually plan out everything that will go into the chapter. They just sit down and write. It should be noted that you can get away with this when you're an experienced writer. If you're not that experienced in the topic itself, you can use other books on a similar subject as a starting point.

As you write, you may find that some ideas don't mesh well with the topic or other chapters in the book. So, you may choose to eliminate it from the book. Additionally, you may choose to deviate from your plan. This means that your instincts and knowledge will help you determine what to keep and what not.

Once you are satisfied with the direction a chapter has taken, you can review it to ensure it represents your idea. If needed, changes can improve the chapter. Otherwise, leaving the chapter as is, will help you move on. The aim is to progress as much as possible.

**Figuring Out Your Word Count**

This is one of the most common questions novice writers encounter. Determining the word count for a book is not always easy. However, there are parameters that you can follow. For example, a 5,000-word book is like a quick guide. At first, 5,000 might sound like a lot, but the reality is that it is not.

Additionally, a 10,000-word book is suitable for an introduction to a topic. Books ranging from 10,000 to 20,000 words offer a good level of detail into a specific topic. Books with a 20,000-to-30,000-word count are rather complex books. They generally require more content given their word count. Anything above 30,000 words is a voluminous book. At this level, you may have to really broaden your scope, or break down the topic into a very high level of detail. In the end, this level of detail will enable you to take up space you need to fully discuss the outcome.

Another good way of figuring out your word count is by looking at other similar books on the same topic. The size of the book can give you an adequate indication of how many words you might need to cover your ideas.

**Sketching your Outline**

Now that you have your chapters and content figured out, it's time to draft up your outline. Having an outline is essential to writing a book as soon as possible, and as accurately as possible. While it's true the some of the best writers are poor organizers, the fact is that you can't afford to be sloppy. As you gain more experience, you might be able to get past this limitation. However, novice writers would do well to write their outline.

A simple organization scheme can be using numerals for chapter numbers and bullet points for the subtopics. Then, you can consult your outline as you progress through the content. This is an important point as having a clear path for your book will lead you to successfully complete it.

Consider this sample outline:

1. Chapter 1: Introduction to the Stock Market
   a. Definition of the stock market
   b. Types of markets
   c. Products traded on the stock market
   d. People involved in the stock market

In this sample outline, we defined one chapter with four subtopics. The next step is to figure out the word count. You can do this by determining how much detail you wish to provide. If you aim to provide only general ideas, then 1,000 words might be enough for this chapter. However, if you want to really dig deep into the subject, you might find that 2,000 to 3,000 words might be more than enough.

You can follow this same system for all chapters in your book. In the end, you'll have a neatly polished outline for your book. It is often said that with a good outline, a book writes itself. This is true because having a good outline eliminates guesswork. As such, all you have to worry about is writing down the information you wish to communicate.

So, please take the time to think about how much content you wish to cover and how you intend to break it down. Doing this will save you time and headaches further down the road.

# Chapter 5: Step 5 - Establishing Credibility Through Research

In the non-fiction world, credibility is crucial. After all, you cannot expect to be taken seriously if you're not careful with the information you put forth. Often, publishers and writers make sensationalist claims just to sell more books. However, these claims, if unfounded, can land you in serious trouble. Nevermind that your books won't sell, you can get sued. Therefore, it is important to conduct research effectively. That way, you can use these sources to back up any claims that you make as part of your publications.

When conducting research, it's a good idea to use the best practices implemented by academic writers. In academic writing, virtually everything you say must be backed up by some kind of credible source. This is why becoming familiar with research sites and other mainstream publications is a must. Moreover, you cannot expect to be taken seriously if you cite sources from non-credible sources. These sources include private individuals not considered experts, fringe organizations, or any other type of non-respected source.

In this chapter, we are going to take a look at how you can use research and trusted sources to boost your publications' credibility.

**Not All Sources Are Created Equal**

When looking at sources, it's often a question of common sense. For starters, there are organizations and institutions which are widely respected. For example, universities, international institutions, and official government organizations are all sources you can rely on. By citing information from these sources, you can back up the claims that you make in your works.

Perhaps the hardest part of conducting research is gaining access to these sources. This can be a challenge if you don't know where to look. So, let's take a look at the places where you can find the information you need.

- *Google Scholar.* This is the first stop for anyone looking to find credible sources on virtually any type of content. Google Scholar is a search engine that is dedicated specifically to finding academic articles published in major magazines and journals, while also offering books and articles.
- *Academic databases.* There are specific academic databases that are widely used by researchers. The best example of these is JSTOR. You can find a plethora of information there. However, please note that you may have to purchase a subscription to these databases if you want to have unlimited access.
- *Journals.* Most major fields of research have dedicated journals. These journals publish articles on topics related to

these fields of research. Since the vast majority of these journals are peer-reviewed, the publications in them are considered to be trustworthy. So, always search for journals on your chosen topic. Most back issues are freely available though you may have to purchase current editions.

- ***Subject matter experts***. A subject matter expert is a respected individual who is recognized for their expertise in a given area. Citing them is a great way of making your points come alive. You can cite interviews, articles, and lectures given by these individuals. So, always check out who the relevant experts are in your specific subject.

- ***Institutional information***. This type of information is generally posted by governments, international organizations, or private companies. Therefore, the information officially published by these institutions constitutes a real position you can use to back up your claims. For example, the United Nations publishes official positions on any number of subjects. As such, you can confidently use the United Nations as backing for the information you present.

Please bear in mind that virtually all of this information is freely available. So, all you have to do is take the time to do the research. While going to your local library still works well, you will find that using the power of the internet makes the research a lot faster and easier.

## Using Disclaimers

Many writers use disclaimers as a means of warning readers that they are only publishing opinions and not making official recommendations. This is important, especially when you're not licensed to advise on a specific matter. For example, you can write a well-researched book on a health issue. However, if you're not a licensed practitioner in that field, you can get sued for the use readers make of that information. So, it's a good idea to include a disclaimer in which you free yourself of such responsibility.

Also, writers and publishers use disclaimers to make it known that the information they provide is for "entertainment purposes" only. Again, this type of disclaimer is widely used in areas that may constitute a risk for the publisher. So, it's always best to double-check if you need to include such disclaimers. A good rule of thumb is to include one whether you need it or not.

That being said, having a well-researched book will help you avoid being criticized for providing senseless information. As such, you can encourage readers to check out the sources you have presented. In that way, readers can take your analysis plus sources to derive their own conclusions.

## Making Citations

Another important element to presenting your research is the use of citations. Depending on the nature of your publication, you can use simple citations such as, "according to…" or "in the opinion of…" These citations are used to introduce the source from which you have derived your information. Moreover, they are used in-text to inform the reader about where the information is coming from.

If you choose, you can use a specific citation format such as MLA, APA, or Vancouver. These types of citation methods are dependent on the type of content. For instance, MLA is used in most academic areas of research. Its defining characteristic is the use of footnotes at the bottom of the page. The APA format is the most used and can be implemented for any type of publication. The Vancouver citation method is mostly used within the medical sciences. Nevertheless, you can choose to use this format if it works best for you.

Ultimately, it's important to use a specific citation format, especially if you're looking to present a more academic paper. Most non-fiction books don't need such a level of detail. Nevertheless, it's always a good idea to put your best foot forward. This level of detail is used by professionals who are looking to position themselves as subject matter experts in their respective fields.

## Being Careful with Plagiarism

Plagiarism is a sure-fire way of getting you banished from the face of the Earth. For instance, Amazon has very strict guidelines about how much duplicate content you can use. Generally speaking, you cannot upload a book that has more than 5% duplicate content. Therefore, a copy and paste approach is not going to cut it. While other platforms may let this slide, there is a very good chance you'll get called out on it eventually.

Plagiarism is considered fraud. While it may not get you in jail, it will automatically get you discredited. Once you are officially discredited, getting back into the good graces of readers is practically impossible. Therefore, you must be very careful about what information you use, and how you use it.

This is why the best way to go is to cite information that you use while limiting the use of direct quotes. Often, writers like to quote other speakers and writers directly. However, this may get you a strike for duplicate content. So, it's best to use direct quotes sparingly.

The best way to use information and quotes from other speakers and writers is to paraphrase. Paraphrasing means writing someone else's words in your own. For example, something like "in the words of Mark Twain…" can be a useful way of ensuring that you present the information you want without getting nailed for improper use.

Please bear in mind that plagiarism is the absolute worst thing you can do in the non-fiction world. So, it's best to ensure that you have the proper citations and give credit when it's due.


**Working Around Plagiarism**

Some unscrupulous folks simply rewrite other established materials. While this is perfectly legal, it's considered unethical. This is especially important if you're serious about positioning yourself within your respective field. There is nothing wrong with paraphrasing other stuff. Just make sure you follow proper citation guidelines.

Now, let's assume that you simply rewrite other material and publish under a pen name. That will do the trick. However, you will quickly find that most readers will catch on to your scheme. So, they may end up punishing you by leaving negative comments and bad reviews. Please keep in mind that bad comments are just as bad as being exposed to academic fraud. As such, ensuring that you always produce the best possible material is a must.

Lastly, please ensure that other writers you work with are on the same page as you are. While you will surely adhere to proper guidelines, you may not be so sure about others. If you suspect that other writers are fudging the rules, please make sure to call them out on it. If you fail to do so, your reputation may get tainted through no fault of your own.

# Chapter 6: Step 6 - Understanding Subgenre

Genre is often at the center of discussion regarding successful non-fiction writing. Mainly, the discussion centers on getting the genre right. While that may seem relatively obvious, it isn't quite as straightforward as you might think. Defining a genre can be tough, especially if you're new to writing.

To define your book's genre, you must be first clear about what you're going to write. This is a crucial first step in determining your book's genre. Next, you need to have a clear vision of your book's scope. From there, you can safely determine your genre. Of course, that is easier said than done.

So, let's take a look at how you can define your book's genre and subgenre accurately. Best of all, you'll find that it's much easier than you think.

**What Is Genre?**

In essence, genre refers to the main topic of a book. This implies that you must have a clear sense of what your book is about. Now, in this book, we're dealing with one main, overarching genre which is non-fiction. As such, your book would most likely fall under the non-fiction genre.

While that's a great start, it's worth noting that such a description is too broad. Therefore, we must dig a little deeper and refine your book's genre and subgenre.

It's also important to note that genre encompasses rather extensive topics. These topics may cover a lot of different aspects. Yet, these are the main topics that readers will look for. From there, they may narrow down their search. This is why first appealing to a broad audience is key. From there, you can narrow your book's focus.

Please bear in mind that your book's genre should be reflected in its title. After all, your book's title will lead readers to find your content. So, you must make sure to include all the relevant words in the title. It will just make it easier for readers to find your work.

**What Is Subgenre?**

A subgenre is a narrower breakdown of your book's topic. In essence, it is the result of further refining your content. When you refine your content further down, you can come up with some rather specific topics to cover. As a result, you must ensure that your overall topic encompasses a clear subgenre.

Main topics such as knitting, gardening, personal finance, or home decoration are all too broad. Therefore, you must narrow your book's focus down to a clear perspective. This is why understanding your book's scope is so important. When you have a clear scope, then it's feasible for you to really drill down on the content you wish to cover.

Please keep in mind that the biggest mistake most novice writers make is leaving their scope too broad. Therefore, they have a tough time focusing on what they really want to say. If anything, they may find themselves bouncing all over the place. When that happens, there is no telling where the book may end up. This is why many writers begin working on a book, but never finish it.

**Reflecting Genre and Subgenre in Your Book's Title**

When selecting your book title, you must ensure that your genre and subgenres are adequately portrayed. In that regard, it can make an enormous difference between having a successful publication and a subpar one.

Consider this situation:

You have just completed a book on living room design. So, you choose to title it, "The Ultimate Living Room." This title is good, but it's a little too vague. Yes, you're reflecting on the fact that the book is about a living room. However, it doesn't tell the reader much more than that. Therefore, the book title doesn't make much sense.

In this case, a better title would be, "The Ultimate Living Room: 25 Great Decoration Ideas for a Small Budget." This title, while longer, encompasses everything you are looking to explain in this book. As such, any reader that comes across your book will know exactly what to expect. Consequently, this book title is much more effective when compared to the first one.

Please keep in mind that your clear understanding of your genre and subgenre must be stated in the title. Given the fact that there is a number of books on any number of topics, you need to make sure that yours stands out as much as possible. The best way to do this is by being absolutely clear about your genre in the title.

**Improving Searchability**

When you have a clearly defined genre, subgenre, and title, you drastically improve searchability. This is key regardless of the platform on which you sell your books. For example, if you sell your books on Amazon Kindle, readers search for topics based on keywords. These keywords are representative of the topic they are looking to read about. As such, you need to make sure that you have the right type of context in mind.

Now, the use of keywords is always important when looking to boost your book's marketing and sales. Keywords must therefore be used within the title. In the previous example, we were clear about including the terms "living room," "decoration," and "ideas."

Why?

Think about it for a minute.

Chances are that a reader would search for a book on this topic under the terms "living decoration ideas." In that case, you would have a clearly defined search. If your title represents these search terms, then you have automatically improved your book's chances of being discovered.

This is also true if you're selling your materials on your website. Your title can be discovered by Google. Therefore, it must reflect your genre and subgenre appropriately. This, in turn, will give search engines the opportunity to find your content amid tons of other types of content and materials.

Experienced writers know that visibility is paramount to successful content. By improving your searchability, you give your content a fighting chance to stand out. What searchability does is give your content a chance to shine through. Therefore, you have the opportunity to become successful based on your merits. Otherwise, great content may get lost in the shuffle. Needless to say, that is the last thing you want.

**Thinking Big**

When you have a clear idea of your genre, you can potentially break it up into an endless number of subgenres. This is important when looking at the bigger picture. The reason for this is based on the fact that you can create an entire series of books based on a general topic. From there, any number of specific subgenres can help you provide all types of readers options to choose from.

Let's consider this example.

You plan to write a series of books and sales and market. Since this is a broad topic, there are potentially endless types of books you could write. So, your job now becomes too narrow things down. For example, you could write a five-part series focused on sales and marketing for small businesses, startups, solopreneurs, online businesses, and family companies.

In this example, you took a broad topic, sales, and marketing, and then broke it down into five more specific topics. In the end, you were able to make the topic work effectively by creating a series of books. Now, instead of having one large volume divided into five parts, you have five separate volumes.

What's the advantage here?

The advantage is that you can boost your sales by appealing to a broader customer base, offering more selections, and focusing on specific market niches. For instance, a person who is interested in sales and market for small businesses would be interested in purchasing the volume dedicated to that topic. In contrast, if you had one volume with five topics, that interested reader may pass as your book contains topics they are not interested in.

Do you see how powerful this approach can be?

Ultimately, your goal is to leverage your writing skills so you can produce a greater income. In the end, you can do that with the same amount of effort. The only difference is that you are using your talents in a much more productive way.

Please keep in mind that you need to have a pretty good idea as to the genre and subgenre of your content even before you write a single word. While it is certainly possible that things can change along the way, it's also important to keep in mind that having a clear starting point can make the difference between a successful book and a disappointing one.

There is no question that you have what it takes to produce highly successful content. So, it's a question of focusing it appropriately. In that case, it will make your job that much easier. That's why it's important to give yourself a hand. Rather than make things harder than they have to be, you can improve your chances right from the start. So, make sure you have a clearly defined genre, subgenre, and title. When you put them all together, you'll have a recipe for a successful book or even a series of books.

# Chapter 7: Step 7 - Building a Winning Formula

At this point, we have laid out the groundwork needed to build a winning formula. This winning formula is about developing a system that can help you become the most successful writer that you can.

Now, it's important to note that this isn't a magic formula. As such, this isn't something you can pull out of a box and let it roll. This winning formula is a highly personalized one. This means that you need to develop a keen understanding of the various elements discussed in this guide. From there, you can create a system that will help you deliver successful content time and time again.

So, we are going to dedicate this chapter to bringing everything together so that you can build a personal winning formula. From there, you will discover just how effective writing can truly be.

**Playing to Your Strengths**

This is pivotal. All writers have personal wheelhouse. That means there are topics and content that they are much better at than others. Therefore, play to your strengths, especially in the early going.

As you make a name for yourself, you want to put your best foot forward. As such, playing to your strengths makes perfect sense. For example, if you're a finance expert, then go down that path. Sure, it might be really exciting to think about writing the next great novel. However, the idea here is to build momentum. By building your momentum, you build your self-confidence. That is what gives you the ability to branch outside your comfort zone.

Also, please keep in mind that readers want value as much as possible. So, using your area of expertise to its fullest potential makes sense. Doing so will put you in a position of strength. In contrast, branching out into other areas may put you in a tough spot. So, playing to your strengths is always the best approach.

With time, you can venture outside the box. You can try working on other topics that you have always wanted to. By then, you'll already have a strong foundation beneath you. Consequently, you'll have the confidence to help you put your best foot forward. As a writer, your experience will help you figure out what works and what doesn't.

So, don't be afraid to go on the power play early on. Eventually, you'll have the experience you need to try new things out.

**Use Your Voice**

Throughout this guide, we've talked about being yourself. This is so true, especially when you're playing to your strengths. Using your voice is crucial when it comes to building rapport with your readers. Believe it or not, readers can pick up when you're trying to be someone you're not. Readers can tell by the way the words flow or don't.

You see, writing is a skill that is honed over time. It's part of an author's thought process. So, the challenge in writing is to organize your thought process in such a way that it's logical and coherent. That will lead readers down a path they can fully comprehend.

It's also important to keep in mind that inexperienced writers tend to produce well-written, but disjointed and incoherent text. Therefore, the challenge becomes to articulate your ideas clearly.

How can you articulate your arguments?

Use your outline!

Yes, when you use your outline, you can produce high-quality content that can lead you to focus your thoughts clearly and coherently. An outline helps you narrow your scope while keeping you on track. Otherwise, you run the risk of simply ranting on about personal experiences or things you know about. While this is useful to a certain degree, all successful books need to have a clear narrative.

Of course, you might hear some writers saying that sticking to outlines can be highly restrictive. That is true to some extent. It requires a lot of experience to simply write without any kind of formal outline, concept, and objective. As you gain experience, it's always a good idea to have a clearly defined concept.

One other thing. Please avoid trying to do everything in your head. When you try to do everything in your head, thoughts can often get muddled and confused. This can lead you to get stuck at any point in your book. So, make sure you write everything down. While it is totally possible to make changes, keeping a written record helps you establish the path you wish to take your readers on. Think of it as building a roadmap before setting out on your journey.

**Stick to a Specific Narrative**

There are some truly gifted writers out there. They can produce quality content on a number of topics. They can write about practically anything. That's both blessing and a curse.

You see, writers often become known for a specific type of genre. Think about all of the great fiction writers. They end up getting typecast into a specific genre because they are successful in it. As such, they focus their energy on that genre. After a while, they don't venture out into other genres, not because they don't have the talent, but to avoid confusing readers.

For instance, let's assume you have made a name for yourself in the medical field. People know you as a great health care professional. Naturally, people would be happy to see you produce content on health and wellness. Over time, you gain quite a bit of traction in this field. Then, you realize your lifelong dream of writing a novel. However, your readers are confused. You're known as a great healthcare professional. So, why are you writing a novel?

Do you see the point in this argument?

Now, it should be noted that lots of folks decide to make a 180-degree turn and write a novel. Also, some folks choose to write about topics they love. That's all well and good. The point is to choose a topic and run with it. Who knows, this could truly put you on the map.

Once you make a name for yourself, you must then commit to that genre. That way, your popularity, and success can just compound with each piece of content you publish. Eventually, you'll have the right following around you.

**Branching Out into Other Genres**

So, what if you can write about other genres?

In that case, it's best to go with a pen name. This is what all great writers do. You see, once a writer becomes known for a specific genre, they have no choice but to go with it. That's why adopting a pen name makes sense.

By taking on another personality, you can ensure that readers will not be biased by your previous success. In fact, some readers may be skeptical about your ability to be successful in other topics. Therefore, using a pen name can remove that bias from your readers' minds.

There is one significant upside to using a pen name. If for some reason, your content flops, your usual reputation won't take a hit. In a way, this takes the pressure off writing new content. For instance, if your first novel flops, you can simply learn from the mistakes. As such, it won't count against your current standing with your followers. This is one of the biggest advantages that writing offers good authors.

The downside to this is that you'll be practically starting from scratch. Your new persona won't have any kind of following. Therefore, you'll need to put in the time and effort to properly market your new content. Nevertheless, your previous experience can help you market your new content effectively.

As your new genre gains momentum, please keep in mind that you may need to eventually come out as the genius behind the magic. Nevertheless, you won't have to worry too much about that. Since your new content has gained popularity, readers will be impressed, not confused.

## How Much Should You Write?

This question gets asked all the time. Many novice writers don't know how much they should write. Also, new authors don't have a sense of how often they should publish new material.

Well, there is a short and long answer to that question.

The short answer is that you should publish new material whenever you have it ready. This means that if it takes you six months to write a new book, then publish it then. Additionally, if it takes you two years to write one, then your audience will have to wait for you that long. Of course, you shouldn't take decades to come up with new material.

The long answer is that you should publish material when it's prudent to do so. For example, let's say that you published a highly successful book three months ago. Since you are a prolific author, you already have two more books in the final editing phase. So, you plan to publish as soon as the next one is ready.

That can be a mistake.

Why?

You see, successful authors publish new content until the sales of the previous ones have stalled. When sales stall, it means that everyone who wanted to read your book has already done it. So, it's time for something new.

Other writers like to follow a specific tempo. For instance, they publish a new book every six months, or once a year. If this sounds like you, it could be a good approach. After all, if your readers get used to your writing tempo, you may find yourself building a steady income stream.

In the end, your winning formula is about building a system that works for you based on good practices. You will find out what works for you soon enough. So, take the time to discover what works for you. Sometimes, you simply have to learn from your mistakes. However, the result will be totally worth it!

# Conclusion

Thank you very much for taking the time to complete this guide. We hope that you now have a great sense of how to write non-fiction content. At this point, you should be able to understand how you wish to pursue your writing endeavors. Mainly, it's about ensuring that you have a system that can lead you to become a successful writer.

So, please take the time to go over any of the concepts provided in this guide. Repetition is a very important part of learning. As such, reviewing previous lessons is always a great way of ensuring that your knowledge has been fixated in your mind. Moreover, review and practice will help you become the best writer you can possibly be.

Often, developing great skills is a question of time. While we would all love to magically flip a switch, the fact is that most of the skills we learn in life come as the result of years of work and practice. Please keep the 10,000-hour rule in mind. This rule states that we need about 10,000 hours of practice before we can truly master a skill.

Now, does that mean that it will take you 10,000 hours to become a great writer?

Not necessarily.

What this idea means is that you need to put in the time and effort to become a successful writer. The more time and practice you put into your writing endeavors, the better you will get. Naturally, this approach means that your success is proportional to the amount of work and sacrifice you are willing to put in.

Please take this opportunity to truly allow your efforts to shine through. You already have the most important elements you need to be successful. So, it is just a matter of making your efforts become a testament to the hard work you are prepared to invest in. The difference between mediocre writers and great ones is the amount of effort and dedication put into their craft. The best writers in history were able to combine hard work and natural talent. Ultimately, this combination has led to some of the most famous works.

Good luck and happy writing!

# More by Jaiden Pemton

Discover all books from the Creative Writing Series by Jaiden Pemton at:

bit.ly/jaiden-pemton


Book 1: *How to Write Fiction*

Book 2: *How to Tell a Story*

Book 3: *How to Write a Screenplay*

Book 4: *How to Write Sales Copy*

Book 5: *How to Edit Writing*

Book 6: *How to Self-Publish*

Book 7: *How to Write Non-Fiction*

Book 8: *How to Write Content*


Themed book bundles available at discounted prices:

bit.ly/jaiden-pemton